Clear Your Doubts About Islam

50 Answers to Common Questions

Compiled by

Ṣaḥeeḥ International

Table of Contents

Foreword

General

1. What is Islam?
2. What is a Muslim?
3. Isn't it true that Islam is an Arab religion?
4. Isn't Islam just another faith based on legends?
5. Don't all world religions have similar objectives?

Religious Beliefs

6. Do Muslims worship God or Allah?
7. If Islam opposes idol worship, why do Muslims pray to a square structure?
8. What is the purpose of worship and why should people worship at all?
9. Why only one God? Could He not create another God like Himself?
10. What is the purpose of our creation?
11. How do you know there is life after death?
12. Why should someone be a Muslim? Can't we follow any religion we please?
13. Are the good deeds of non-believers rewarded?
14. Isn't Islam fatalistic?
15. Are there sects in Islam?

Prophets and Scriptures

16. Who was Muhammad?
17. Do Muslims worship Muhammad?
18. Why should Muhammad be the final prophet? Haven't there been others after him?
19. Didn't Muhammad write the Qur'an or borrow from the earlier scriptures?
20. How does the Qur'an differ from other scriptures?

21. Is it true that Muslims don't believe in Jesus? What does Islam say about him?

Legislation
22. What is Shari'ah?
23. What are the "pillars" of Islam?
24. Why is alcohol prohibited?
25. Why is pork prohibited?
26. Why do Muslims allow the slaughter of animals?
27. What is the Islamic view on abortion, suicide and "mercy" killings?
28. Why does Islam oppose homosexuality? Where is freedom of choice?
29. Doesn't Islamic law encourage vengeance?
30. Why does Islam demand harsh punishments for sex outside marriage?
31. Why is a woman's share of inheritance half that of a man?
32. Why is the testimony of two women required in place of one man?

Social and Family Issues
33. Isn't Islam intolerant of other religions? How do Muslims treat people of other faiths?
34. What is Islam's attitude toward Western civilization today?
35. Why is so much of the Muslim world underdeveloped?
36. If Islam is such a good religion, why do we find many Muslims dishonest, unreliable and lazy?
37. What is Islam's view about education, science and technology?
38. Does Islam accept slavery?
39. Is there any mention of human rights in Islam?
40. Doesn't Islam oppress women?
41. Are men and women considered equal?

42. Why does Islam keep women behind the veil?
43. Why is a Muslim man allowed to have more than one wife?
44. Why does Islam prohibit a woman from having more than one husband?
45. How can a Muslim be happy?

Warfare and Terrorism

46. Why are so many Muslims fundamentalists and extremists?
47. Doesn't Islam promote terrorism, making it a threat to the world?
48. Wasn't Islam spread by the sword?
49. Isn't Islam a militant religion?
50. What is the meaning of jihad?

Finally .....

References

21. Is it true that Muslims don't believe in Jesus? What does Islam say about him?

Legislation
22. What is Shari'ah?
23. What are the "pillars" of Islam?
24. Why is alcohol prohibited?
25. Why is pork prohibited?
26. Why do Muslims allow the slaughter of animals?
27. What is the Islamic view on abortion, suicide and "mercy" killings?
28. Why does Islam oppose homosexuality? Where is freedom of choice?
29. Doesn't Islamic law encourage vengeance?
30. Why does Islam demand harsh punishments for sex outside marriage?
31. Why is a woman's share of inheritance half that of a man?
32. Why is the testimony of two women required in place of one man?

Social and Family Issues
33. Isn't Islam intolerant of other religions? How do Muslims treat people of other faiths?
34. What is Islam's attitude toward Western civilization today?
35. Why is so much of the Muslim world underdeveloped?
36. If Islam is such a good religion, why do we find many Muslims dishonest, unreliable and lazy?
37. What is Islam's view about education, science and technology?
38. Does Islam accept slavery?
39. Is there any mention of human rights in Islam?
40. Doesn't Islam oppress women?
41. Are men and women considered equal?

42. Why does Islam keep women behind the veil?
43. Why is a Muslim man allowed to have more than one wife?
44. Why does Islam prohibit a woman from having more than one husband?
45. How can a Muslim be happy?

Warfare and Terrorism

46. Why are so many Muslims fundamentalists and extremists?
47. Doesn't Islam promote terrorism, making it a threat to the world?
48. Wasn't Islam spread by the sword?
49. Isn't Islam a militant religion?
50. What is the meaning of jihad?

Finally .....

References

Foreword

No one can deny that Islam is very much in the spotlight today. In spite of extremely negative portrayals by western media or perhaps because of them, increasing numbers of people are seeking to find out more about it. And more often than not, they are being pleasantly surprised by the fruits of their research. In fact, more people are embracing Islam today than they did prior to September 11, 2001.

However, there does remain a great deal of misconception and misunderstanding on the subject, frequently fueled by political policies which deem it in their interest to support Islam's enemies. In addition, Muslims themselves, at first shocked and confused by the events of recent years, did not really know how to respond to the challenge. Now they have been rudely awakened to the urgency of refuting the many false claims and accusations being spread against their way of life and of defending the truth, and accordingly, the rights and honor of Muslims everywhere on earth.

Islam is the religion and way of life of about one fifth of the world's population. Muslims are of diverse nationalities, cultures and races, but their religion teaches that all men are essentially equal and that no distinction should be made between them on the basis of such superficial differences as color, class status or personal beliefs as long as they remain peaceful and law-abiding citizens. The behavior of certain misguided groups or individuals outside the fold of mainstream Islam cannot be attributed to the religion any more than violence in North Ireland or Mafia activities can be attributed to Christianity.

People of secular cultures often fail to understand why practicing Muslims cannot always fit in completely with modern westernized lifestyles, why they insist upon a particular type of dress or upon prayer at particular times. They tend to perceive Muslim attitudes as unnecessarily demanding and uncompromising. Misunderstandings are frequently due to unmistakable differences between the western concept of religion and that of Muslims. Islam can indeed seem strange to a society in which religion no longer plays a major role in everyday life; but to a dedicated Muslim, Islam *is* life, and there is no division between the secular and the sacred.

Because religious practice occupies a narrow place in his outlook, the adherent to western culture often does not comprehend the relationship between a Muslim and his religion or what motivates him to take a particular direction in life. But in the view of Islam, religion is not merely a personal issue or something symbolic pertaining to a limited area of one's existence. On the contrary, it involves molding a balanced way of life suitable not only to Muslims but to everyone who inclines toward peace, justice and respect for rights. More simply, it can be said to mean the pursuit of happiness, security and moral perfection. In the hearts of Muslims, their religion remains both a secure refuge and the most effective motivator for tackling all kinds of challenges. At the same time, it preserves the distinctive character of the Muslim believer and the pattern of his particular culture.

An individual in the west might see religion within a limited context pertaining to worship alone – a private matter between a person and God. But in Islam, it is a dynamic system that organizes the progression of life according to basic general principles and flexible rulings that guarantee potential benefit from advancements in science and technology as well as new material facilities. Since there is no conflict between Islam and scientific research, every new discovery in the world of matter, energy, time and space only increases the believer in faith and humility towards Him who devised, projected and systematized such a plan and then assigned to mankind his place and noble role within it. Within this understanding, it remains to be said that knowledgeable Muslims are not in need of secularism since they have no problem with religion.

It is hoped that by putting out accurate information in greater quantities, the world will eventually come to know Islam as it really is and not as portrayed by its adversaries. It is toward this objective that Ṣaḥeeḥ International has produced a booklet providing answers to the questions most often raised by non-Muslims of the present day. We also invite our readers to find out more about Islam by contacting the nearest Islamic Education Center, bookstore or library.

General

1. **What is Islam?**

"Islām" is an Arabic word which means peaceful, willing submission – submission to the code of conduct ordained by God. So Islam is a religion, but it is also a complete way of life based upon a voluntary relationship between an individual and his Creator. It is the way of life ordained by God which was taught by each of His prophets and messengers. What distinguishes Islam from other religions is that it refuses to accept any form of creation whatsoever as a deity worthy of worship. Instead, it emphasizes the exclusive worship of the one God who created the entire universe and to whom all creation will eventually return.

Monotheism is the foundation of Islam and its most important concept which cannot be compromised in any way. Not only is God acknowledged as the sole creator and sustainer of everything in existence, but Islam declares that He is the only true deity and He alone is worthy to be worshipped. Further, it recognizes that the attributes of God are nothing like those of His creation and cannot be compared to it; He is absolute, perfect and unique.

2. **What is a Muslim?**

A Muslim is someone who practices Islam; that is, who willingly submits to the revealed directives of God. Everything in the universe is inherently submissive to God, functioning according to the natural laws created by Him. Human beings are physically "muslim" in that their bodies function according to the genetic program set by God for the period of time He has decreed.

A "Muslim" in the religious sense, however, is someone who consciously commits himself to the worship of God alone, not according to his own inclinations or those of other men but according to the method conveyed by God through His appointed prophets. The Qur'an gives many examples of people who lived before Muhammad who believed in and obeyed the prophet that God sent them and thus entered Paradise, because that is the meaning of "Islam."

All the prophets of God, from Adam to Muhammad, and those who believed and followed each of them during the period of his prophethood[1] were called "Muslims." But since Prophet Muhammad was the last of God's messengers to mankind, a "Muslim" can now only be defined as one who accepts and complies with the final, completed message conveyed by God through him. For rationally, the most recently revised legislation always supersedes and invalidates whatever came before it.

3. Isn't it true that Islam is an Arab religion?

This mistaken assumption is possibly based on the fact that Prophet Muhammad was an Arab, that most of the first generation of Muslims were Arabs and that the Qur'an is in the Arabic language.

But in actual fact, only about 18 percent of Muslims in the world today are Arabs. The largest Muslim populations are found in Indonesia, the Indian sub-continent and other parts of Asia. Islam is also widespread in many parts of Africa and there are substantial minorities in Europe, North and South America and Oceania. Islam is the fastest growing major religion in the world, and its adherents on all continents include both Arabs and non-Arabs.

---

[1] i.e., until another prophet was sent after him.

Further, not all Arabs are Muslims, for there are significant communities of Christian Arabs as well as a number who belong to other religions or profess atheism. While "Arab" is a geographic and cultural term, "Muslim" refers to an adherent to the religion of Islam.

While the revelation was still in its early stages, the Qur'an disclosed that Islam is indeed a global religion. Allah addressed His Prophet therein, saying:

"And We have not sent you but as a mercy to [all] the worlds."[2]

"And We have not sent you except comprehensively to mankind, as a bringer of good tidings and a warner, but most of the people do not know."[3]

Islam is meant for all people regardless of race, nationality, cultural or religious background. From the commencement of his mission, the Prophet's companions came from a wide range of lands and races. Among them was an African, a Byzantine, a Persian and a Jewish scholar. All were united in the brotherhood of faith.

There are many references in the Qur'an to the universal nature of Islam. It frequently addresses humanity, saying, "O mankind" or "O people." The Prophet, his companions and their followers made every effort to spread the message of truth to all nations and peoples. He naturally began the propagation of God's message among his own people, the Arabs, but that does not mean it was restricted to them – rather, only that initially conveying it to those nearest him was the logical first step toward the realization of a long term goal. Later in his mission when conditions became more favorable he sent letters of invitation to Islam to the

---

[2] 21:107.
[3] 34:28.

rulers of Byzantium, Persia, Abyssinia, Egypt, Damascus, Bahrain, Yamamah, Oman and others who represented the influential world figures of the day. Whatever their response to it, the Prophet's message was fully acknowledged by the major powers of his time.

4. Isn't Islam just another faith based on legends?

On the contrary, Islam is the only religion whose sources are authentically preserved, historically recognized and have remained entirely free of human alteration and interference over the centuries. Its divine scripture, the Qur'an, contains no myths or fables and is in accord with established facts of science. It provides an acceptable explanation of the origin, development and purpose of the universe and for occurrences within it.

The message of Islam is not new. What is new is the form of the message, its dimensions and scale. This final revelation has been preserved in its original state, as promised by God when He revealed:

"Indeed, it is We who sent down the message, and indeed, We will be its guardian."[4]

It has miraculously remained immune to the ravages of time and the interference of man, and is still accessible in its original language to all who seek guidance.

Distinct from the teachings of many religions which assume the incompatibility of faith and reason, Islam upholds the role of the mind and regards those who fail to use reason as intellectually deficient. Because the mind tends to seek out interrelationship wherever there is variety and multiplicity, it is satisfied by the Qur'an's clear and

---

[4] 15:9.

unambiguous statement that everything is traceable to a single source, backed with sound arguments and evidence. An important feature of Islam is that while it is based exclusively upon revelation from God, never exceeding the bounds of the divinely revealed texts, it does not fail to provides logical proofs for its tenets.

Islam teaches that one should expect a natural cause for everything that occurs in creation. It promotes the research, study, thought and contemplation that leads one to faith by conviction rather than blind acceptance. The Qur'an urges man to observe and consider the signs of God within creation and provides guidelines for the sound thinking that leads to appropriate conclusions.

5. Don't all world religions have similar objectives?

There are many areas in which religions agree but there are also significant theological and practical differences between them. Undeniably, one will find in every religion expressions of wisdom, high moral values, warnings against evil and promotion of good works. But what distinguishes Islam from other faiths is that it goes beyond simply urging people to be generous and morally upright. Islam identifies human problems and prescribes practical solutions to them, both individually and collectively.

Although there are a variety of religious communities in the world, each of them content with its own version of "the truth," Islam represents the completion of divinely revealed religion and the finalized legal code for mankind. For this reason the Qur'an states:

Verily, the religion in the sight of God is Islam.[5]

---

[5] 3:19.

The divine messages revealed prior to that of Prophet Muhammad all called for the worship of God alone and contained some legislation. However, each of them was addressed to a specific people at a specific period of time in order to remedy particular problems and circumstances such as moral degeneration, economic injustices and excessive materialism, misuse of power and political oppression. The final message of Islam addresses these same social evils, but as part of a comprehensive program for the amendment, reform and benefit of every nation, community and individual that will exist until the end of the world.

The prophethood of Muhammad launched an era in which divine guidance became openly universal, more comprehensive in scope and precisely detailed. The responsibility for man's fate and moral well-being depends completely on his own free choice and willing initiative to respond to the invitation of his Creator.

Religious Beliefs

6. **Do Muslims worship God or Allah?**

One of the biggest misconceptions about Islam concerns the name "Allāh." Some people believe that Muslims worship a different God than Christians, Jews and others, and some missionary organizations distribute literature in English in which they say such things as: "Allah is the god of the Muslims" and "Muhammad told people to believe in the god, Allah." They thus imply and reinforce the idea that "Allah" is some sort of false deity.

This is totally incorrect because "Allāh" is the same word that Arabic-speaking Christians and Jews use for God. If you pick up an Arabic Bible, you will find the word "Allāh" wherever "God" is used in English. "Allāh" is also the proper name of God. Therefore Muslims use the name "Allāh" even when they speak other languages.

"Allah" is a special word. It indicates the only entity in existence who truly possesses the qualities of divinity and lordship, the Creator and Sustainer of the heavens and earth. It is the name of the only being worthy of worship, the one upon whom all creation is dependent at every moment. This name belongs to God alone and no one else.

"Allāh" is the only word in the Arabic language equivalent to "God" with a capital "G." It is also a unique word grammatically since it cannot be made plural or given a masculine or feminine gender. This is consistent with the Islamic concept of God. In English and other languages the word "god" can be used in various forms such as "God", "gods" or "goddess," all with different connotations and meanings. The only difference between "god," meaning a false god or any object of worship, and "God", meaning the one true God, is a capital "G." Thus, a more accurate translation of "Allāh" might be "the one and only true God."

But there is another important point, which is that Islam is particularly concerned with the correct concept of God. Someone can have an erroneous concept of Him whether he uses the name "Allāh" or the word "God." Followers of previous religions gradually deviated from the original pure belief in God due to the fact that their scriptures were not adequately protected from loss and alteration. None of these are still available for study in their original form or language.

But this is not true of the last divinely revealed message, the Qur'an. Hence, the accurate concept of God can be found therein.

7. **If Islam opposes idol worship, why do Muslims pray to a square structure?**

The simple cube shaped stone building located in Makkah is called the Ka'bah or the Sacred House. It is the point toward which Muslims face when they pray. Although Muslims face the direction of Ka'bah during prayer, they do not worship it. Muslims worship and pray only to God.

The Ka'bah was built by the prophet Abraham and his son, Ishmael in response to God's command over 4000 years ago. Abraham consecrated the House for the worship of the one true God and invited all of humanity to visit it for that purpose. Even today Muslims who are physically and financially able are required to make a pilgrimage to it once in a lifetime. The Ka'bah has remained at the center of a continuous tradition of worship and devotion up to the present day, symbolic of permanence, constancy and renewal.

There were periods in human history during which mankind deviated from the monotheism taught by God's prophets. Before the advent of Muhammad religion among the Arabs had degenerated into polytheism and paganism and Makkah was completely submerged in idolatry; some 360 idols had been placed in and around the Ka'bah to be worshipped there along with God. Prophet Muhammad was sent to restore to mankind the pure monotheism taught by all the messengers of God and reinstate the worship of Him alone. This he accomplished, and the Ka'bah was finally cleared of all man-made deities.

Among the ancient religious rites particular to the Ka'bah is walking around it. This suggests the integrating and unifying power of monotheism in human life and how a Muslim's existence should revolve around a pure devotion to God. The Ka'bah symbolizes the unity of all true religion, the brotherhood of all the prophets and the essential consistency of their message.

When Muslims pray facing toward this single central point they are reminded of their common purpose and long term goal. Even when standing directly before the Ka'bah in prayer one is not to look at it but rather at the ground before him. The spiritual focus is on God alone and never upon any created object.

8. What is the purpose of worship and why should people worship at all?

The idea of servitude has become distasteful to the modern secular mind-set which concerns itself with individual liberties. Some might say that humanity has no need to worship, and that doing so compromises freedom. They forget, however, that absolute freedom is neither possible or even desirable for all members of a society, and that is why every social order has its laws and restrictions.

Studies in human psychology confirm that that man is a worshipper by instinct, that worship is instilled in him as part of his nature and that he tends to direct it to whatever he considers worthy – other human beings, revered customs or superstitions, materialist ideologies or his own personal inclinations. An object of worship is that to which one devotes the greatest portion of his thought and effort. So one either worships God or he worships something other than Him – along with Him or instead of Him. The worship of God alone is liberating in that it frees one from servitude to all else.

Many people misunderstand the concept of worship, assuming that it is merely the practice of certain rituals. But in reality it includes everything done seeking the acceptance of the one worshipped. According to Islam, the worship of God means willing obedience to His orders and prohibitions which, besides prayer and other religious obligations, include the fulfillment of promises and agreements, honesty and precision in work, teaching and counseling, encouraging righteousness, assisting others, opposing injustice and so on.

Worship is the right of the Creator upon His Creation. It is based on the perception that everything was brought into existence by God and is dependent upon Him in whose hand is life and death, benefit and harm and the outcome of every matter. Further, it is based on the knowledge that man is an accountable being in need of God's continuing guidance and acceptance. Islam confirms that although it is His divine right, God does not gain anything from the worship of His servants, nor is He harmed by their refusal. He ordains worship for the benefit of the worshipper himself and this benefit is obtained by him or her in both this life and the next. When a believer understands that our Creator and Sustainer deserves to be worshipped he wants to do so because of his gratitude, and love for his Lord and because it is inherently right and correct.

9. Why only one God? Could He not create another God like Himself?

The implication here is that the existence of dual or plural deities is possible and hence probable in the view of a polytheist. However, if the questioner claims that God can create another like Himself we ask, "How can this created being be God, who created all things, when it has itself been created? How can it be like God since it has a beginning whereas God has existed from eternity? In reality, the phrase "create another God" is an erroneous contradiction, because the mere fact that something is created means that it cannot be God. It is obviously illogical and irrational to say that something is God and cannot be God simultaneously.

The other implication in this question is that if we answer, "He cannot," then the power of God must be limited, negating His divinity. These suggestions are not valid because the absolute and unlimited power of God pertains to what is rationally possible and not what is rationally impossible. So when we say no, which is correct, it does not mean that the power of God is limited. Rather it affirms the perfection of His power, meaning that He is not incapable of doing anything that is rationally possible.

Our minds cannot grasp the extent of His power, nor can our imaginations. Therefore, we must admit our inability to contain the essence and nature of God within the limits of our intellect.

10. What is the purpose of our creation?

Non-believers are unable to provide any convincing reason for the existence of this universe or of human life. People who believe there is a Creator assume that creation occurred by His will. But in a world where everything is shown to have a purpose, it is natural for a human being to wonder about the purpose of his own creation. One is surely justified in expecting the Creator who put us on this earth to inform us why He did so and what He expects of us.

The Qur'an informs us that He did just that. It says that God created us for a test here on earth. And it conveys His words:

"Then did you think that We created you uselessly and that to Us you would not be returned?"[6]

A non-believer might decide that the objective of his life will be to collect wealth, obtain position or pursue pleasure to the greatest extent possible. But none of this will benefit him in the long run. According to His final scripture, God created man to test him with certain responsibilities.[7] He did not intend life on this earth to necessarily be comfortable or satisfying, but merely a trial of limited duration, the punishment and rewards of which will be due in the Hereafter.

As mentioned previously, most of creation is "muslim" in that it is programmed to obey the physical laws set by God, and this is why the universe functions with balanced equilibrium. Man, however, was given a free will and the ability to either obey or disobey. But God will not allow His universal balance to be upset indefinitely by defiant, corrupt and sinful people, so He only grants human beings a measure of freedom in a temporary world. The scheme of birth, development, decline and death provides each with the opportunity to prove to himself without a doubt what he will deserve on the Day of Judgement, which God created for the manifestation of His ultimate justice.

This life is very meaningful and purposeful to the believing Muslim because he realizes that it will determine his outcome and permanent position in the next life. He lives to earn the approval of his Creator in preparation for the final return to Him.

We all recognize that people make things to perform specific functions for them, in other words, to serve them.

---

[6] 23:115-116.
[7] As stated in 18:7, 67:2 and 76:2.

God has made us to serve Him, but with one major difference; it is not for the benefit of the Creator Himself, but for the benefit of us, His creation. The purpose of our existence is thus stated in the Qur'an:

"I did not create the jinn and mankind except to worship Me." [8]

But man's worship of God it is not automatic like the vast majority of created beings, but by his own choice and effort, and this is what entitles him to honor and reward.

How should one worship God in order to fulfill that purpose?" This question can undoubtedly best be answered by Him. God has provided every element of His creation, living and inanimate, with guidance. We can thus expect that He would provide us with guidance as well. His revelation instructs humanity what to do, what to avoid and the reason for it. It informs man what is expected of him, how to accomplish it and the results of continual positive effort. Through Prophet Muhammad, God revealed to man the ways of worship suitable to his physical and psychological nature and individual talents and in harmony with his particular role on the earth. These, in combination, are what enables him to fulfil the purpose of his creation.

11. How do you know there is life after death?

We live in a world that demands logic and proof and is not content with only belief. Someone might wonder how a rational, practical minded person could believe in life after death. People tend to assume that anyone who believes in the Hereafter does so on the basis of blind faith. But in fact, belief in the Hereafter is completely logical. And it is the only way the injustices of this world can be reconciled with a just and all-powerful Creator.

---

[8] As stated in 51:56.

We know that in addition to physical pleasures and comforts there are certain ideal conditions that human beings instinctively desire and strive to attain, such as love, respect, security and contentment. Though many people are able to acquire a portion of these objectives here on earth, there remains one that is largely unobtainable – and that is justice. Most people hold the conviction that life is not fair: that they have often been misunderstood or not appreciated, that in some way they have been harmed, cheated or oppressed. Daily newscasts disclose the killing, torture, displacement and starvation of countless innocent people by powerful tyrants and nations, lives ruined by the vicious or careless acts of others or by natural disasters, and the poor and helpless being subjected to theft and deception. Seldom is even partial justice ever restored. Yet, every human being desires justice. Even if he does not seek it for others he certainly wants justice for himself.

So why has the Creator instilled in man a longing for something he cannot experience in this world? The answer is that this life is only one portion of his existence and that the logical conclusion which restores the equilibrium found in all creation is in the Hereafter. It is there that every person will be fully and precisely compensated for his good and evil deeds. This is the perfect and absolute justice which God has promised all people.

The present life is a trial in preparation for the next realm of existence. The explanation given by the Qur'an about the necessity of life after death is what the moral consciousness of man demands. If there was no life after death, the belief in God would be meaningless, or it would be a belief in some kind of indifferent and negligent deity who, after having created the human race, is no longer concerned with its welfare.

But certainly, God is just. He will indeed punish the tyrants who have killed thousands and caused suffering to their families, corrupted institutions and societies, enslaved people and nations, robbed, deprived and plundered. And what about those who patiently endured so much injustice and hardship, suffered to uphold truth, saved lives or sacrificed in order to assist many people? What earthly compensations could possibly restore the balance for them?

This can only take place in an eternal life where every individual affected in the least by someone's actions will testify for or against him, and where the innermost thoughts and intentions, known completely to God, will be judged precisely and perfectly. Since man's term of life in this world is limited and because numerous individuals are affected by one's actions, adequate rewards and punishments are impossible in the present life. The Qur'an states categorically that the Day of Resurrection must come and that God will then decree the fate of each soul according to its record of deeds.

Additionally, God has stated in the Qur'an that the present creation is in itself a clear proof that He is able to create and re-create as He wills, whatever He wills, however He wills and whenever He wills, for God originates and repeats creation with equal ease. Consider these words revealed to His final Prophet:

> *Say, " Travel through the land and observe how He began creation. Then Allah will produce the final creation."*
>
> *Did We fail in the first creation? But they are in confusion over a new creation.*[9]

---

[9] 50:15.

Is not He who created the heavens and the earth able to create the likes of them? Yes, and He is the Knowing Creator.[10]

Do they not see that Allah, who created the heavens and earth and did not fail in their creation, is able to give life to the dead?[11]

Does man not remember that We created him before, while he was nothing?[12]

And you have already known the first creation, so will you not remember?[13]

Have they not considered how Allah begins creation and then repeats it? Indeed that, for Allah, is easy.[14]

And it is He who begins creation; then He repeats it; and that is easier for Him.[15]

As We began the first creation, We will repeat it. [That is] a promise binding upon Us. Indeed, We will do it.[16]

In fact, the material of creation is already in existence, merely to be developed once again at His command. Observable evidence of this ongoing process is now being presented regularly by astronomers and specialists in other fields of modern science.

12. Why should someone be a Muslim? Can't we follow any religion we please?

---

[10] 36:81.
[11] 46:33.
[12] 19:67.
[13] 56:62.
[14] 29:19.
[15] 30:27.
[16] 21:104.

There are many people who follow the teachings of a religion as best they can and others who believe in God in some way without practicing any formal religion.[17] Many have abandoned the thought that there could be any true religion because nearly all religions claim to be true. And some allow that all religions are legitimate paths to God and are acceptable to Him. So how is Islam different from other religions?

Islam has several unique features which can be confirmed through deeper study:

- Islam is the only religion whose sources have remained free of human alteration and interference.
- Its divinely revealed scripture is in harmony with established facts of science, clearly bearing the signature of the Creator of this universe.
- Islam provides answers to the essential fundamental questions which occur to the mind of every intelligent person, those related to the purpose of creation and life and concerning a further existence after death.
- Islam is the only religion which insists upon worship of the Creator alone and completely rejects the worship of any aspect of creation.

---

[17] Anyone to whom God's message was not adequately conveyed, yet believed in Him and tried to worship Him with sincere intention will be judged by God according to what is in his heart and mind, for He is the ultimate judge of all affairs. The Quran states that God never punishes a people until after He has sent them a messenger with the clear order to worship their Creator alone without any associates. It also states that He does not punish for what people are unable to know or what is beyond their capability.

- Islam dispenses with all intermediaries between man and God and allows every individual to contact Him directly, thus eliminating religious hierarchies and other sources of exploitation which have characterized the history of religions throughout the ages. In Islam no cleric or establishment can come between a person and his Creator.
- While monotheistic faiths share a fundamental belief in God, their understanding of Him differs greatly. Islam declares that God is unique and in no way similar to any of His creation; nor does He merge with it in any form. His attributes are those of complete and absolute perfection without the slightest deficiency or limitation.
- Unlike other religions and ideologies which emphasize some aspects of human nature at the expense of others, Islam accommodates the physical, intellectual and spiritual aspects of man. Islamic beliefs and practices are natural and appeal to common sense. They present a balanced program of life that fulfills both physical and spiritual needs.
- Islam prohibits blind following without knowledge and is based upon evidence and logic. The rational mind is the basis for religious accountability and responsibility. All aspects of Islamic belief are clear, without any obscurity or ambiguity. It contains no tenet that contradicts reason or observable reality, and it calls on people to study and contemplate as a means of strengthening faith.
- Islam's religious, moral, economic, political and social ethics are permanent and remain constant. They are governed by a set of unchanging principles which include such universal values as justice, freedom, equality, brotherhood and social responsibility. History provides an outstanding example in the model Islamic society established by Prophet Muhammad and his companions

and maintained for decades by devoted Muslims, where truth and transparency, justice and compassion were implemented and as a vital expression of the religion.

Islam also declares that it is the religion of truth, for this is stated unambiguously in the Qur'an. However, the Creator does not force His preference on anyone. He wants people to accept right guidance by their own choice and free will because that is what makes them worthy of His approval and reward. The Qur'an states:

There is no compulsion in [accepting] religion. The truth has been made distinct from falsehood.[18]

Had Allah willed, He would have made you one nation [united in religion], but [He intended] to test you in what He has given you; so hasten to [all that is] good. To Allah is your return all together, and He will [then] inform you concerning that over which you used to differ.[19]

13. Are the good deeds of non-believers rewarded?

Prophet Muhammad disclosed that God rewards according to the intention of each individual. The non-believer expects to be rewarded for his deeds in the present life because he denies or doubts the existence of another life after his death. Thus, he is keen that people should recognize what he does; when he is praised and his deed publicized he is pleased, for this is the reward he sought. He might also obtain a sum of money in payment for it or a prize. This is the compensation he likes most and God grants it to him. But he is not given additional reward in the Hereafter simply because he neither desired it nor worked for it.

---

[18] 2:256.
[19] 5:48.

The believer, on the other hand, is not duly concerned with compensation in this life because he is striving for the greater eternal reward of the Hereafter. He does so by worshipping God as He stipulated and by working patiently, honestly and correctly to the best of his ability, even when no person appreciates his efforts. Because his deeds are done seeking God's acceptance they are appreciated by Him and rewarded.

Islam teaches that there are two conditions for God's approval and reward of any deed: (1) that it is done explicitly for His acceptance and approval and (2) that it is consistent with the methods ordained by Him. In other words, a person must work for God according to the terms He has specified and not according to his own preferences or those of other people. In order to know exactly what God expects of His servants it is necessary to refer to the legislation revealed by Him in its final form through Muhammad, the final prophet.

14. **Isn't Islam fatalistic?**

Muslims know that all things are from God and occur by His will. Thus, they tend to worry less about material matters and view the life of this world in proper perspective. A Muslim believer relies completely on God and knows that whatever happens is always for the best, whether he recognizes it or not, so he graciously accepts whatever cannot be changed.

However, this does not mean that a Muslim sits around awaiting destiny and takes no positive action in life. On the contrary, Islam demands action and effort to change every undesirable situation and this is a requirement of the faith. It totally rejects the teaching that one should not go to a doctor when ill but only pray to God for cure. If human beings had no ability to act God could not justly expect them to do and not to do certain things. Far from being "fatalistic," Islam teaches that man's main obligation in life is to exert effort in obedience to God, which includes seeking benefit and avoiding harm.

Islam teaches that human beings should take positive action in life and supplement it with prayer. Some people are lazy and careless and then blame the negative result on destiny or fate. Some even say that if God had willed they would not have sinned or committed crimes. All this is entirely incorrect because He has provided complete guidance and instruction on how to live and has ordered upright conduct at all times. God has not ordered anything that man cannot do or prohibited anything he cannot avoid because His justice is complete and perfect. Each individual is held responsible within the limits of his own ability, but not beyond it.

Although our deeds and our destiny are decreed by God and known to Him, it does not mean He compels us to do anything. Rather, He willed to give us options about our course of action; and thus, whatever decisions we make are within the framework of His will. God knows what every person will choose to do and then allows him to do it, while not necessarily approving of his choice. While He does not call anyone to account for what is beyond his control, human beings are indeed responsible for every free choice they make, and they will find the consequences of their choices and actions in both this life and the next.

"Cause and effect" is a natural law created by God to be utilized by His creatures. It is the law by which one's destiny is determined. So the destiny of each individual is predetermined by God, but it is also the direct result and consequence of his or her own choices and actions, and this is what the Creator has willed and decreed.

15. **Are there sects in Islam?**

Islam is one path, has one direction and is based on one methodology – that which Prophet Muhammad taught according to the instruction he received from God. The religion God ordained for mankind was meant to be a unifying factor. In fact, He addressed mankind in the Qur'an, saying:

" And this is My path, which is straight, so follow it, and do not follow [other] ways for they will separate you from His way." [20]

This divine command emphatically makes it binding on all Muslims to be united as one community of believers; thus, all forms of schism and sectarianism are un-Islamic.

The Prophet's companions and following generations adhered very closely to the path of God, and thus He protected them from separating in this manner. But with later generations certain factors led to the emergence of divisions and divergence, among them: increasing concern with worldly affairs, the influence of non-Muslim cultures and political rivalries. Initially, some small groups split off from the path adhered to by the majority of Muslims. They introduced innovations into the religion and followed opinions differing from the original teachings of the Prophet.

These schisms were rejected and opposed by the recognized scholars of Islam and the majority of Muslims, which meant that initially they were contained and that their influence did not become widespread during the major part of Islamic history. The majority of Muslims remained on the Sunni[21] path, and whenever forms of deviation emerged

---

[20] 6:153. The subtle change in the verse from first to third person expresses the progressive process of distancing oneself from God's path.

[21] A Sunni is one who takes his religion from the Qur'an and Sunnah, i.e., the authentically narrated teachings of Prophet Muhammad as practiced by him and his righteous followers.

among them the pious scholars always hastened to oppose them and point out their error.

Prophet Muhammad foretold that such divergences would emerge. He warned against schism and instructed Muslims to remain within the main body of Islam.

Nevertheless, over the centuries a number of people have deviated and corrupted their religion, forming sects that claim to belong to Islam but whose stated beliefs are clearly contrary to it. Some have distorted the concept of God and attributed to Him what is unfitting or incompatible with His divine status – claiming, for example, that everything in existence is God or that He is incarnate or present within His creation, while the Qur'an states that He is superior to His creation and distinct from it. And some have been misguided regarding various major tenets of Islam to the degree that they no longer submit to God and obey Him, while others have innovated and changed some of the prescribed forms of worship.

Those sects which deviated from mainstream Islam are not the same as the schools of Islamic jurisprudence[22] which developed within it and are based on the immutable principles of the faith. These eminent schools of thought have provided a vision of the highest degree of scholarship for Islamic legislation and serve to complement one another. Differences and disagreements within the framework of Islam do not become matters of partisanship and intolerance except among the extremely ignorant.

Islam recognizes the individuality of human beings and that not all diversity of opinion and difference in analysis is

---

[22] The Hanafi, Maliki, Shafi'i and Hanbali schools and a few others less known.

negative. However, the kind of dissension that leads to schism and sectarianism has been denounced in the Qur'an:

Indeed, those who have divided their religion and become sects – you, [O Muhammad], are not [associated] with them in anything. Their affair is only [left] to Allah; then He will inform them about what they used to do.[23]

Although Muslims now appear to be divided more than ever before, the number of divisions in Islam remain fewer than in other religions. One can still find many Islamic associations calling people to truth, proclaiming God's original message and warning against that which is contrary to it. Salvation does not depend on affiliation with any specific group, but rather on true faith proven by obedience to God and upright conduct in the manner revealed by Him.

Prophets and Scriptures

16. Who was Muhammad?

Muhammad bin Abdullah was a descendant of Prophet Abraham though his son, Ishmael,[24] and was from the prominent Arab tribe of Quraysh. He was not the founder of Islam but its final prophet and the last messenger sent by God to the world as a mercy to mankind. Every detail of his private life and public speech has been documented and carefully preserved up to the present day.

---

[23] 6:159.
[24] Isaac, another son of Abraham, was the ancestor of the Children of Israel, among whom a number of prophets were raised.

During the 23-year period of his prophethood he changed the entire Arabian Peninsula from paganism to worship of the one true God, from tribal warfare to national unity, from anarchy to disciplined living, from barbarism to the highest standard of moral excellence. At the time of his death most inhabitants of Arabia and the southern regions of Iraq and Palestine had voluntarily embraced Islam. To posterity he left a creed of pure monotheism that included comprehensive legislation based on a balanced system of moral values.

No other man in history excelled in so many different aspects of life. He not only taught and established the religion, but founded a state, initiated numerous political and social reforms, built a powerful and dynamic society and completely revolutionized the realm of human thought and behavior – all within just over two decades.

His coming was foretold in previous scriptures and he was described therein. The honest and open-minded among the Jews and Christians recognized him from those descriptions and believed in his message. But the message he communicated was not meant for a particular people, place or period; it was a global message. Muhammad was appointed to instruct all of mankind and invite humanity to the same objective as did the prophets before him: the worship of God alone without associates or intermediaries.

There is explicit evidence for the prophethood of Muhammad. As the revelation descended upon him his companions noticed certain effects on his body; however, he never lost consciousness or showed any signs of illness. His life was protected by God during times of severe danger throughout the entire period of his prophethood until the divine message was complete. Like the prophets before him, Muhammad was supported with miracles, but by far the greatest of them was the Qur'an, an eternal miracle containing evidences for people of intellect for all time to come.

Prophet Muhammad was chosen by the Creator of the universe and of mankind to invite all people to correct beliefs and the pure way of life preferred by Him, and to demonstrate the measures and methods leading to His acceptance. He spared no effort and no sacrifice in carrying out this duty for the benefit of mankind. Through him, God made known truth from falsehood and wisdom from error. And through him He showed man how to attain eternal Paradise. Thus, Prophet Muhammad directed humanity to the one divine source of values and rules of conduct.

17. Do Muslims worship Muhammad?

Islam is based on uncompromising monotheism. God alone is to be worshipped and nothing else, so Muslims cannot worship Muhammad or any other human being.[25] Like all prophets, he was a man, and despite his extraordinary accomplishments he never claimed divine status. Rather, he always maintained that he was human like everyone else, that he spoke nothing of his own accord, and that the Qur'an was a message from God, revealed to him by God, to whom alone belongs all glory and praise. He never took personal credit for any success. All the principles he taught, the legislation he pronounced and the great achievements for which he could have attained personal renown and advantage were attributed to the guidance and support of God alone.

---

[25] The basis for this misconception actually comes from the early orientalists who called Islam "Mohammedanism," implying that Muslims worship Muhammad.

Muslims strive to follow the example of Prophet Muhammad. Additionally, Islam teaches Muslims to respect all of God's prophets and messengers. However, respecting and loving them does not mean worshipping them, for all forms of worship must be directed only to the Creator.

Muhammad was himself a devout worshipper of God. He gave away everything he obtained in charity, fasted often and would spend a great portion of the night in prayer. He was constantly aware of his Lord, remembering Him in every situation, and his words of praise and supplication reflected the highest degree of sincerity and servitude. His entire life was dedicated to the cause of God. He called on people to worship God alone, and insisted that they refer to him as merely a servant of God, telling his followers, "Do not exaggerate in praise of me as the Christians did with Jesus, son of Mary. I am only His servant, so say, 'the servant of Allah and His messenger.'"

18. Why should Muhammad be the final prophet? Haven't there been others after him?

Prophethood is not something acquired by a person who proves himself worthy, nor is it granted in recognition of piety. Prophethood is an office to which God appoints a man in order to fill a particular need. The Qur'an mentions four conditions under which prophets were sent to the world:

1) When no prophet had ever been sent to a people before and no divine message had reached them

2) When the message of an earlier prophet had been forgotten by the people or the teachings of former prophets had been altered with time

3) When a second prophet was needed to assist a first one

4) When a people had not yet received complete instruction from God

In each of these cases a prophet was appointed to convey divine revelation, updating previous messages and correcting deviations that man had introduced into the religion of God.

After God's message was completed through revelation to Muhammad and its preservation guaranteed, there was no further need for messengers to convey revelation; only for teachers and reformers to remind people of what God had revealed.[26] From the time of Muhammad's prophethood conditions in the world have been conducive to the transmission of God's message to all civilizations, making the appointment of additional prophets unnecessary. This final message has undergone no amendment or alteration by man; not a single word has been added to it or deleted from it.

If God intended to send another prophet after Muhammad, He would have made that fact clear in the Qur'an or commanded His Messenger to declare that a prophet would follow him. But the Qur'an clearly affirms that God has now completed His divine mission through Prophet Muhammad.[27] Therefore, the office of prophethood has been canceled, enabling the world to unite in allegiance to the final prophet and obedience to God. For everyone who accepts Muhammad as the divinely appointed final messenger will seek instruction only within the message he conveyed.

19. Didn't Muhammad write the Qur'an or borrow from the earlier scriptures?

---

[26] The Qur'an says: **"Muhammad is not the father of [any] one of your men, but [he is] the Messenger of Allah and seal [i.e., last] of the prophets."** (33:40)

[27] God stated therein: *"This day I have perfected for you your religion and completed My favor upon you and have approved for you Islam as religion."* (5:3)

Opponents of Islam sometimes allege that Muhammad himself wrote the Qur'an or that he copied or adapted it from previous scriptures. But it is known that the Prophet's contacts with Jews and Christians was negligible before his emigration from Makkah, and after it his role was that of a teacher, openly inviting the Jews and Christians to accept Islam while pointing out how they had diverged from the true monotheism taught by their prophets.

It is true that there are some similarities between the Qur'an and the Bible, but this does not indicate that later prophets plagiarized from former ones. It merely reflects the common source, which is the Creator of mankind, and the continuance of His basic message of monotheism. Moreover, there was no Arabic version of the Bible in existence at the time of Prophet Muhammad. The earliest Arabic version of the Old Testament is that of R. Saadias Gaon of 900 CE - more than 250 years after the death of Prophet Muhammad. And the oldest Arabic version of the New Testament was published by Erpenius in 1616 CE - about 1000 years after his death.

Historically and logically, it cannot be established that there was any human source for the Qur'an or that the Messenger of Allah learned it from the Jews or Christians. His enemies kept a close watch on him hoping to find confirmation of their claim that he was a liar. But they could not point to a single instance when the Prophet might have had secret meetings with people of other faiths.

It was a sign of Muhammad's prophethood that he was illiterate. Thus, he could not be credited with composing or editing the revelations, and suspicion that he learned what he preached from earlier scriptures is eliminated. At the time the Qur'an was revealed, his contemporaries among the Arabs, known for linguistic eloquence, acknowledged that its language was unique and distinctly different from the speech of Muhammad, a man they knew well. The Qur'an states that the Prophet was an unlettered man, so if that had not been true his opponents would surely have exposed him. There is, however, not a single report to this effect, and no one denied his illiteracy. At the same time, no one denied that the Qur'an was unequaled in eloquence, impact and clarity, including those who rejected its message.

It is not difficult to verify that Muhammad did not possess knowledge of many things mentioned in the Qur'an, such as historical events, natural phenomena and future occurrences. The kind of information he conveyed could not have been obtained through reading and research, so it was obviously something that could only have come directly from the Creator. The Qur'an states in several places that Muhammad and his people did not know these facts, so had it been otherwise, his adversaries would have capitalized on that claim to discredit him. Only recently, within the last two centuries, have advancements in research technology led to the discovery of facts that were mentioned in the Qur'an by the unlettered prophet over fourteen centuries ago. Here are a few examples:

- The creation of the universe from a single entity and of life from water: *Have those who disbelieved not considered that the heavens and the earth were a joined entity, and We separated them and made from water every living thing?*[28]

- All creation is based on duality, made up of pairs, counterparts or opposites: *And of all things We created two mates.*[29]

---

[28] Qur'an - 21:30.

[29] Qur'an - 51:49. In contrast, God is one, with no counterpart and nothing resembling Him in any way.

- The different natures of the sun and moon: *It is He [Allah] who made the sun a shining light and the moon a derived light and determined for it phases – that you may know the number of years and account [of time].*[30]

- The rotation of the earth: *He created the heavens and earth in truth. He wraps the night over the day and wraps the day over the night.*[31]

- The expansion of the universe: *And the heaven We constructed with strength, and indeed, We are [its] expander.*[32]

- The sun is not stationary but moves in a specific direction for a limited term: *And the sun runs [on course] toward its stopping point.*[33]

These are words recited by Muhammad, the unlettered prophet. The Qur'an addresses recently established scientific facts with the precision of a scientist. Could the most highly literate, well read or scholarly man of that period, or even of the centuries that followed, possibly have come up with anything similar?

20. How does the Qur'an differ from other scriptures?

The Qur'an was revealed over 1400 years ago. It states in no uncertain terms that it is a revelation from God

---

[30] Qur'an - 10:5. Other verses (25:61 and 71:16) refer to the sun as a burning lamp.

[31] Qur'an - 39:5. The alternate "wrapping" of sunlight and darkness is caused by the earth's turning in one direction.

[32] Qur'an - 51:47. The Creator refers to Himself in the plural form which denotes power, grandeur and majesty.

[33] Qur'an - 36:38. The sun, as a tiny member of this vast universe is progressing within it toward a final destination, which indicates an end to the present creation.

conveyed by the angel Gabriel to Prophet Muhammad. It is regarded, not only by Muslims but by scholars of religion and historians, as the most authentic religious text in existence today. Unlike earlier scriptures, the Qur'an has been preserved unchanged in its original Arabic text since the time of revelation, as God had promised within it.[34]

History witnessed the fulfillment of that promise, for the Book of God remains to date exactly as it was revealed to the Prophet and recited by him. Immediately memorized and recorded by large numbers of his companions, it was passed on in exactly the same form by thousands of Muslims generation after generation up until the present day. The Qur'an of today is literally the same scripture as was revealed to Prophet Muhammad. There is no other book in the history of man that has been memorized precisely and accurately, word for word, letter for letter by millions of people over the centuries. This in itself is a miracle.

There is only one version of the Qur'an; the same revealed words continue to be read, recited and memorized in their original Arabic language by Muslims throughout the world. Translations of the meanings into other languages assist in understanding but cannot be called "the Qur'an," as this term refers only to the actual revealed words of God.

The Qur'an contains God's final message to humanity and legislation which encompasses all spheres of human life. It is suited to all peoples and all times. It appeals to logic, following clear reasoning and citing evidences from the created universe, from history and from the human soul to establish not only the existence of God, but also His

---

[34] Its preservation was guaranteed when God revealed: ***"Indeed, it is We who sent down the message, and indeed, We will be its guardian."*** (15:9) Note: God often refers to Himself in the Qur'an as, "We," which does not denote plurality, but power and majesty.

uniqueness and absolute perfection. It also contains answers to the questions which naturally occur to the human mind about the purpose of creation and what occurs after death.

It is the primary source of the Islamic creed and its legislation. But in addition to religious guidance it contains numerous verses that speak of the universe, its components and phenomena - the earth, sun, moon, stars, mountains, wind, rivers and seas, plants, animals and successive stages of development of the human being. As can be seen from examples in the previous chapter, the Qur'an speaks with the perfect knowledge of the Creator about His creation. Being the final revelation to mankind, God has made the Qur'an a continuing miracle containing evidences to be uncovered gradually as humans increase in knowledge of their universe.

But its main purpose is to guide mankind as to how one should relate to his Creator, to his fellow men and to the universe in general. It outlines the practical methods of earning the approval of God and obtaining peace and contentment in the permanent existence to come. By following its guidance man can fully experience his human worth and his special position among created beings. The Qur'an was revealed containing complete guidance in all matters of faith and its application to the affairs of human life in order that everyone might attain the happiness and contentment of this world and the next.

21. Is it true that Muslims don't believe in Jesus? What does Islam say about him?

One cannot be a Muslim if he does not believe in Jesus as well as all other prophets sent by God,[35] including Adam, Noah, Abraham, David, Solomon, Moses and Muhammad.

---

[35] The Qur'an names twenty-five prophets and messengers and suggests that there were many more.

Muslims have the highest regard for Jesus and await his second coming.

The Islamic view of Jesus is one between two extremes. The Jews rejected his prophethood and called him an impostor while many Christians regard him as the son of God and worship him as such. Islam considers Jesus Christ, the son of Mary as one of the great prophets of God, worthy of respect and honor but not worship. He was sent to confirm and renew the basic doctrine of belief in God, the Creator, alone and obedience to Him.

According to the Qur'an, he was born miraculously without a father.[36] And he was not crucified but raised up to God.[37] The Qur'an attributes to him miracles that are not even mentioned in the Bible. However, Islam sees the deification of Jesus as a reversion to paganism and the divinity of Jesus is categorically rejected within the Qur'an's text.[38] Such doctrines as the "trinity," "divine sonship" and "atonement" are not accepted by Muslims simply because they did not originate from Prophet Jesus himself.

It is known that most of the Gospels were written by men long after the time of Jesus and that much of the New Testament was compiled from the writings of Paul and his students. Unmistakable contradictions have appeared in the various "modern," "revised" and "amplified" versions of the Bible. The once purely divine message conveyed by Jesus has obviously been corrupted by human input and altered through numerous translations; the original texts no longer exist.

The Gospels were written several decades after Jesus' departure and none of their authors had actually seen Jesus or heard him speak. Moreover, they were written in Greek while

---

[36] Refer to Qur'an, 19:16-35.
[37] Refer to Qur'an, 3:55 and 4:157-158.
[38] Refer to 5:72.

Jesus spoke Aramaic. Those Gospels presently in circulation were not selected from among the others and authorized by the Church until the decisions of the ecumenical Council of Nicea in the year 325 CE.

Nevertheless, belief in the divine scripture, not in its present form but as it was originally revealed to Prophet Jesus, is an article of Islamic faith. The final revelation from God is the only criterion by which information in previous scriptures can be evaluated. Therefore, whatever the Bible says about Jesus that agrees with the Qur'an is accepted by Muslims and what is contrary to it is rejected as a product of human intervention.

Legislation

22. What is Shari'ah?

The Arabic word *shari'ah* refers to the laws and way of life prescribed by God for his servants. It deals with ideology, faith, behavior, manners and matters of daily life. We recognize that customs and traditions, good taste and civil law all have some authority over people in every culture, preventing them from doing certain things and obliging them to do others. So it is to be expected that religion, too, would have some authority over people. In Islam, this authority rightfully belongs to God and is derived from His final revelation.

The Islamic Shari'ah is a divinely ordained legal system whose primary objective is benefit to mankind. Its principles are designed to protect people from evil and direct them to what is best in all aspects of life. Moreover, its benefit is for everyone – rich and poor, rulers and ruled, men and women, Muslims and non-Muslims, whose right to worship and manage their personal and family affairs according to their own norms is explicit. The Shari'ah provides injunctions that guarantee justice, promote the general welfare, preserve order, safeguard human rights, and define responsibilities.

Its established constants are derived from the texts of the Qur'an and teachings of Prophet Muhammad, and have been confirmed by a consensus of Muslim scholars both in theory and practice. These basic principles are agreed upon by all, while differences over variables are acceptable and in fact, provide the flexibility necessary for the system to accommodate changing circumstances.

Besides defining methods of Islamic worship, the Shari'ah provides an outline for thought and education based upon such moral values as justice, generosity, chastity, honesty, mercy and respect for humanity in general. It provides the standard for social and political issues – the choice of a ruler, consultation within the government, opposition to injustice, defense of truth and right, individual and collective duties, intellectual enlightenment based on evidences and proofs, respect and tolerance for the viewpoints of others and the encouragement of open and frank discussions.

Generally, anything that is neither known to be harmful nor mentioned as forbidden in Islamic law is permitted. In what pertains to daily life, all is allowed except for was explicitly prohibited in the Qur'an or by Prophet Muhammad, and this includes everything harmful, whether or not it is considered so by limited human perception. What is forbidden in Islam is a small segment of the whole, so that what is permitted is sufficient to make what is forbidden unnecessary. For example, the encouragement and facilitation of lawful marriage greatly reduces the temptation toward fornication and adultery. When Islam forbids sexual relations outside the framework of marriage, the aim is to purify individuals and societies physically and morally. Similarly, interest can be replaced by lawful business gains, gambling replaced by competition in sport and religion, fornication replaced by lawful marriage, and forbidden food and drink replaced by healthy food and drink.

The general purpose and objectives of the Shari'ah do not change. It clearly defines what is prohibited and considers all other things to be permissible. Only harmful things have been prohibited and whatever has benefit has been permitted. Islamic legislation maintains a balance between the needs of the individual and society, allowing neither to outweigh the other.

The inner deterrent of man's moral conscience is fully integrated with external supervision. Islam stresses the role of the individual conscience and is concerned with cultivating within it the fear and love of God and the hope for His mercy. This ensures that an individual will be responsive to the commandments of God even when there is no external monitoring system, and that he or she will voluntarily avoid what is prohibited. However, the system does not rely exclusively upon the conscience. It complements its role by providing laws to be upheld by society and enforced by the judicial authority.

It is true that the system includes a few severe penalties for certain types of criminals, but in practice, crime has always been drastically reduced within societies that applied Islamic Shari'ah, and this is the real purpose of its legislation. Crime and punishment cannot be treated as separate issues. When the Shari'ah is considered in totality, one finds that initially, every measure is taken to provide what is lawful and block all avenues leading to the unlawful. Moreover, punishment cannot be applied unless it is established beyond any doubt that the crime was committed with knowledge of its prohibition and without compulsion by someone of legal age and sound mind. Further, an additional burden of providing trustworthy witnesses in some cases makes conviction highly unlikely. In light of the numerous constraints, a determined transgressor, once convicted in a court of law, may rightly be made an example as a further deterrent to others. Thus the system is not only just, but most merciful to society as a whole.

On another level, the Shari'ah operates to satisfy the sense of justice of the victim and his heirs. Contrary to what some people suppose, there is no capital punishment for murder. Retribution is a legal decision given to the victim's family and carried out by the courts according to their instruction. They have three options:

1. They can demand that the state executes the murderer on their behalf.
2. They can opt instead for a payment of blood money from the murderer.
3. They can forgive the murderer and forgo any kind of compensation.

Forgiveness in this world, however, does not necessarily mean acquittal in the Hereafter. A would be offender is deterred not only by the threat of physical or pecuniary punishments; he is first and foremost accountable before God, who may forgive or punish as He sees fit.

One of the features of Islamic legislation is that it has a moderate approach to issues and problems and regarding the relationship between the individual and society. The Shari'ah has left particular areas open for scholars to make interpretive judgments according to changing norms and circumstances. It responds to the demands of social progress in a way that keeps it compatible with the practical realities of a changing world and reconciles the issue of progress with that of ideological continuity, striking a balance between progress and continuity in matters of human life. At the same time, it maintains continuity in its primary goals and objectives. Its religious, moral, economic, and social values remain constant, governed by a set of unchanging principles.

23. What are the "pillars" of Islam?

The "five pillars" are the main requirements of Islam. Like the pillars of a building, the religion can neither stand nor be completed without them. These requirements are:

1. The declaration of faith

To be a Muslim, one must believe in and pronounce words which mean, "*I testify that there is no deity other than God (Allah) and I testify that Muhammad is His servant and messenger.*" It expresses the belief that God exists, that He is unlike and superior to His creation and that none is worthy to be worshipped but Him. And it confirms that Muhammad is among the prophets who conveyed God's revelation to mankind. Thus, the Qur'an, being the final message revealed by God, and the authentically narrated teachings of His final prophet are the basis of the religion, completing and superseding all that came before it, and they define the Islamic way of life. It is a declaration by the believer of acknowledgement and willing obedience.

2. The performance of regular prayer

Prayer was practiced in some form throughout history by all the prophets and their followers as an indispensable part of God's religion. Islam, the final stage of monotheistic religion, considers prayer essential. A Muslim prays five times daily within specified intervals, as taught by the Prophet. These prayers are obligatory, and are a direct and continuous bond between the worshipper and his Creator. Most believers are inclined also to pray additional voluntary prayers whenever convenient, as it was the practice of their Prophet.

3. Zakah (obligatory annual expenditure)

An important principle of Islam is that all things belong to God and that all wealth, possessions and properties are held by human beings in trust. Muslims are commanded to obtain and spend their wealth in lawful ways. The divinely ordained system of *zakah* is the right of Allah within His dominion. It is neither a charity nor a tax, but an obligation due from those Muslims who possess wealth in excess of their basic needs. It is the ideal way to meet the needs of the poorer sections of society without causing hardship to the rich. The word "zakah" means purification and growth. Its regular payment purifies the owner's remaining wealth and purifies his heart from such ailments as greed and selfishness. Every Muslim calculates his own zakah individually, and in most cases it involves the payment of two and a half percent of his excess capital or savings each year.

4. Fasting

Islamic fasting, which involves abstinence from eating, drinking, smoking and marital intercourse, is observed throughout the daylight hours of the lunar month of Ramadhan. Done in obedience to God's command, it teaches believers patience and self-control, as well as reminding them of their responsibility toward the millions of human beings who lack adequate food and provisions or are victims of their unjust distribution. The month of fasting is accompanied by increased efforts toward good manners and righteous deeds, along with additional worship at night. It is not a retreat from life but rather, a supplement to the Muslim's ordinary activities.

5. Hajj

Hajj, the annual pilgrimage, is an obligation once in a lifetime only for those who are physically and financially able to perform it. Nevertheless, over two million Muslims journey to Makkah each year from every corner of the globe, providing a unique opportunity for people of various nations and cultures to meet one another as guests of God. Hajj is an expression of pure faith and total submission to His command, and the pilgrim performs rites of unqualified obedience, seeking nothing but the Creator's acceptance of his efforts and forgiveness of his past sins. He returns home with a fresh outlook on life, a purified soul and blessings from his Lord.

24. Why is alcohol prohibited?

In Islam all things which are harmful or whose harm exceeds their benefit are unlawful. This includes every substance that affects the mind, damages it or decreases its abilities. Therefore, alcohol would be deemed unlawful even if it were not clearly prohibited in the Qur'an and prophetic traditions. For anything that causes harm in any way is considered unlawful.[39]

There are a number medical reasons for the prohibition of the consumption of alcohol. Alcohol has been the scourge of human society since time immemorial. It continues to take countless human lives and cause misery to millions throughout the world. And it affects the mind, diminishing the individual's mental powers and making him accustomed to running away from his problems. It affects his finances as well, due to the expenditure that his generally

---

[39] Some people claim that they can exercise self-control and never get intoxicated. But investigations reveal that every alcoholic began as a social drinker. No one initially starts drinking with the intention of becoming an addict. It just happens along the way.

expensive habit forces upon him. There is no need to go into detail about all the ill effects of alcohol since most of them are commonly known.

Because alcohol incapacitates the inhibitory center in the brain, an inebriated person is often found to be indulging in behavior that is completely uncharacteristic – using abusive language, becoming aggressive and violent or committing shameful acts. Statistics showing a rising number of deaths, soaring crime rates, increasing instances of mental illness and millions of broken homes throughout the world bear witness to the destructive effect of drinking alcohol.

The harm that results from alcohol is not limited only to the one who drinks; it is also damaging to others. The diseases caused by alcohol weaken society as a whole. Productivity is decreased due to its effects and crimes result from addiction. According to a World Health Organization report on violent crimes in 30 countries, 86% of murders and 50% of rapes are carried out under the influence of alcohol. There are similar statistics in most countries around the world. Additionally, public health officials have estimated that half of the road accidents resulting in deaths and permanent disabilities are caused by people under the influence of alcohol.

Islam agrees that prevention is the best treatment. However, Muslims do not abstain from drugs and intoxicants due to its detrimental effects, but rather, because God has prohibited them. So abstention is a form of worship and obedience for which they are rewarded by God in the Hereafter, as well as protecting them from harm in the present life.

25. **Why is pork prohibited?**

Again, obedience to God in this matter is the primary motivation, while prohibition is based on the principle of avoiding harm. In the Qur'an as well as the Bible, pig flesh has been forbidden and declared unclean. Regarding the physical harm caused by eating it, modern medicine has confirmed a number of facts, such as the following:

- Pork is a kind of meat that contains much cholesterol, which is known to increase the likelihood of blocked arteries.

- The pig's meat and fat have been found to contribute to the spread of cancers of the colon, rectum, prostate and blood. Eating it has been connected to scabies, allergies, stomach ulcers and lung infections.

- Eating pig flesh has been connected to no less than fifty other diseases. Among them are the infections caused by roundworms, pinworms, hookworms and tapeworms, whose eggs, when present in the meat, are ingested by humans, enter their blood stream and can reach and damage almost all organs of the body.

- A common misconception is that if pork is cooked well, the worm eggs are destroyed. But in a research project undertaken in America, it was found that the ova present in pork do not die under normal cooking temperatures.[40]

- It is also known that some diseases such as rheumatism and joint pain are unique to humans and pigs, and are not shared by any other animals.

Muslims accept whatever legislation has been issued by God out of conviction and complete trust in the knowledge and wisdom of the Lawmaker.

---

[40] In particular, the trichinosis worm is not destroyed by cooking. Its growth in the body can cause infection of the cerebral membrane and brain, the heart muscle, the lungs, kidneys or nerves.

26. Why do Muslims allow the slaughter of animals?

This question is often posed by vegetarians, advocates of animal rights and some Hindus. In fact, there are people who consider the consumption of meat to be a violation of animal rights. But meat is not forbidden to Muslims.

While Islam enjoins mercy and compassion toward all living creatures, it maintains that God has created plant and animal life for the benefit of humankind. Man has been ordered and entrusted by the Creator to use every resource in this world judiciously because it is a blessing from Him and a trust.

Islam offers one of the most humane methods of animal slaughter. The objective of Islamic slaughter is to ensure minimal pain and maximal blood drainage from the animal as detrimental microorganisms flourish in blood. Besides Muslims, people from other ethnic and religious backgrounds are assured that meat slaughtered Islamically is healthy and of high quality. It remains fresh for a longer period due to the lesser amount of blood in the meat in comparison to other methods of slaughtering.

Animals are slaughtered in a swift and merciful manner with the pronunciation of words meaning, "In the name of God; God is Most Great." This acknowledges that the animal's life is being taken with God's permission to meet the lawful need for food. The Islamic mode of slaughtering an animal also requires that the following conditions be met:

- The animal has to be fed as usual prior to slaughter and given water.

- It may not be beaten or tortured in any way by man or machine. Stunning before slaughter is not permitted.[41]
- One animal should not be allowed to see another being slaughtered.[42]
- The knife should be large enough and razor sharp.
- Slaughtering is done from the front of the neck and the butcher must swiftly sever the respiratory tract, esophagus and jugular vein without cutting the spinal cord. With swift cutting of the blood vessels in the neck at the proper place, rapid and profuse bleeding causes instant shock and anesthetization in the brain so that no sensation is felt. Thus, the animal does not suffer.[43]
- The animal must be completely lifeless and the blood drained completely before skinning and removing the head.

The promotion of healthy and correct methods of food production is part of the Islamic way of life. Its legislation encourages a strong respect for the sanctity of life and an abhorrence to cruelty to animals.

27. What is the Islamic view on suicide, "mercy" killings and abortion?

A true Muslim is satisfied with himself and his place in the universe due to the knowledge that he is not merely a worthless particle within an accidental existence or an insignificant creature with no purpose or role to play in life.

---

[41] This is accomplished by use of a bolt pistol, electric shock or electrified water (in the case of poultry), all of which cause additional stress and suffering to the animal.

[42] In an authentic narration by at-Tabarani, the Prophet scolded a man for even sharpening his blade while the sheep was watching him.

[43] The Prophet instructed, "Allah has decreed proficiency in all things. So when you slaughter, slaughter well. Let each one of you sharpen his blade and spare suffering to the animal he slaughters." (Narrated by Muslim)

He knows that he is a chosen servant of God, holding a position of honor, trust, favor and responsibility. He is certain of his Lord's perfection, all-encompassing knowledge and absolute wisdom, justice and mercy. He knows that nothing is created without purpose, and that God's favors and blessings are infinite and beyond human perception.

Islam emphasizes the value of human life. It also teaches that one should not despair of God's mercy and recognize that His decree is always beneficial in some way, even when it might seem otherwise. The endurance of pain, discomfort or hardship while accepting God's decree is something that benefits a Muslim in the Hereafter and increases his reward. Prophet Muhammad said, "No tiredness, exhaustion, worry, grief, distress or harm befalls a believer in this world, not even a thorn that pricks him, but that God expiates some of his sins thereby."[44]

Suicide indicates impatience and a lack of trust in God. It is thus prohibited to Muslims and considered among the major sins that is subject to the will of God on the Day of Resurrection; He may either forgive it or punish for it.

So-called mercy killings come under the same ruling. Although painkillers may be prescribed for those who are terminally ill or badly injured, it is not allowed to use or be given medications that are known to cause death either sooner or later. A basic principle of Islamic Shari'ah is that harm cannot be removed by something else that is equally harmful, so it is not permitted to use medications that will cause greater harm than the disease itself, which is the taking of a human life without a legally just cause.

As for abortion, it is unlawful in Islam to terminate a pregnancy at any stage unless there is a justifiable reason, and

---

[44] Al-Bukhari and Muslim.

then, only within very precise limits. If the pregnancy is within the first forty days and aborting it serves a legitimate purpose or will prevent harm, then it is permissible to do so. But fear of difficulty in raising children or maintaining and educating them or the couple's belief that they already have enough children is not a permissible justification for abortion.

After four months it is not lawful to abort a pregnancy unless a group of trustworthy specialists decide that keeping the fetus in its mother's womb will lead to serious medical consequences or threaten her life. Even then, it may only be done after all means of eliminating the danger and keeping the fetus alive have been exhausted. In this case the concession allowing abortion is made in order to avert the greater of two evils or serve the greater of two interests.

28. Why does Islam oppose homosexuality? Where is freedom of choice?

In the West today, homosexuality and lesbianism have come to be seen as an alternative life style subject to personal preference. It is no longer considered an abnormality that requires restraint and treatment, and is being actively promoted by its adherents and their sympathizers as a legitimate way of life. Arguments in favor of tolerance toward same sex relationships are based on the assumption that homosexual behavior is biologically based and not merely learned from society.

Islam considers homosexuality to be the result of human choice. Human beings are not robots that do only what they are programmed to do. They choose how to behave, and God holds them responsible for their choices. It is inconceivable that God would have made some people homosexuals then declared it a punishable crime.[45] To accept such a proposition is to suggest that God is unjust.

Inclinations can exist within humans toward a variety of natural acts and unnatural ones such as rape, pedophilia or bestiality. These inclinations may arise from media influence or direct contact, but it does not mean that free reign should be given to them. Muslims are under obligation to control and overcome such inclinations in obedience to God.

It should be noted that Islam did not introduce anti-gay legislature to the world. The texts of the Torah are replete with clear condemnation of such practices. But among the things foretold by the Prophet of Islam is this: "Immorality will not appear among a people to the extent that they publicize it but that painful diseases will spread among them which were not known to their predecessors."[46]

Sexually transmitted diseases are steeply on the rise in permissive societies – in particular, HIV/AIDS, which causes loss of acquired immunity and usually leads to death. The early spread of AIDS was first observed among homosexual communities. Later, it entered the heterosexual community through so-called bisexuals as well as blood transfusions and intravenous drug usage, and now it continues to spread among promiscuous heterosexuals. AIDS remains incurable and infections continue to increase in gay and bisexual men, who accounted for more than half of HIV infections in 2006.

Islamic teachings emphasize the distinctions between male and female. Islam instructs parents to separate their

---

[45] God has created everything in due proportion. He established the means for populating the earth and maintaining life by the creation of male and female, not only in man but among most all living things. Islam considers deliberate efforts to change this nature as rebellion against the Creator.

[46] Narrated by Ibn Majah and al-Hakim.

children in their beds by the age of ten in order to avoid sexual experiences which may result from childhood experimentation. Such experiences are often reinforced by contacts in school or through abuse from perverted adults. Islam also encourages early marriage in order to facilitate lawful sexual relations for young people as soon as possible and keep them away from unlawful and unnatural ones.

29. Doesn't Islamic law encourage vengeance?

Islam is often accused of having legislation that encourages retaliation rather than forgiveness. But the Qur'an itself refutes this, saying:

> *But whoever overlooks from his brother [the killer] anything, then there should be a suitable follow-up and compensation to [the victim's heir] with good conduct. This is an alleviation from your Lord and a mercy.*[47]
>
> *And the retribution for an injury is one like it, but whoever pardons and makes reconciliation – his reward is [due] from Allah. Indeed, He does not like the unjust.*[48]

Justice is the ruling spirit of Islamic law. However, the changing definition of terms such as "civilized", "freedom" and "equality" have resulted in criticism of Islamic laws and the argument that in view of the changing world, the Shari'ah is outdated. To a believing Muslim, this amounts to denial of the wisdom of God who put us on this earth with a purpose in life and a responsible role to fulfill.

Punishment has always been an integral part in the concept of justice. Islam considers crime an act of injustice towards society as well as a sin. Punishment is not atonement

---

[47] 2:178.
[48] 42:40.

for sin because a sin can only be forgiven through sincere repentance. A crime, however, is the infliction of harm upon others which cannot be forgiven by repentance alone.

The object of all penal systems is to punish the offender and protect society from reoccurrence of the crime. However, if societies were to rely only upon punishment, they would fail miserably. An environment of healthy morality and faith must be the norm, where right conduct is encouraged by all and wrongdoing is opposed and made as difficult as possible.

In Islam, penalties are only part of a larger integrated whole. They cannot be properly understood nor justifiably implemented in isolation. God has ordained a body of mutual rights and obligations. He has also set certain bounds and limits to be observed by everyone for the maintenance of justice. If men and nations want to have peace and safety on the highways of life, they must remain within the "traffic lanes" marked out for them and observe the "signposts" erected along their routes. Otherwise, they endanger themselves and others and thus subject themselves to penalties – not out of reprisal, but in order to regulate and preserve orderly interactions among all people in society.

In many non-Muslim societies today, there are ongoing debates about the death penalty. In Islam the matter has been decided by the Creator, who said:

"And there is for you in legal retribution [saving of] life, O you [people] of understanding, that you may avoid [sin]."[49]

The verse alludes to the fact that such punishments serve as a strong deterrent to crime. They are of a functional nature, to regulate and prevent reoccurrence.

---

[49] 2:179

There are basically three categories of punishment in Islamic Shari'ah: First is *hadd,* fixed punishments for a few specific crimes that were divinely ordained. Second is *qisas* for homicide and assault, in which the victim or family of the deceased has the right to legal retribution or else to accept monetary remuneration or even to pardon the offender, both of which serve to avert capital punishment. The Qur'an highly recommends forgiveness. An injured party may take particular circumstances into account or overlook the offense with the expectation of being compensated by God in the next life. And third is *ta'zeer,* which is a discretionary penalty decided by the court. There are stringent conditions which must be met for any of these to be applicable and strict procedures must be followed before any person can be convicted and punished.

Another important function of these penalties is educational. They are intended to instill in society a deep feeling of abhorrence for transgression against fellow human beings and against God. Once one understands the basic concepts, objectives and framework of Islamic Shari'ah, he cannot but conclude that it is capable of creating the most humane and just society. Difficulties arise only when critics try to measure the ocean of divine knowledge, wisdom and justice with their own imperfect criteria and understanding.

30. Why does Islam demand harsh punishments for sex outside marriage?

As mentioned previously, punishment in Islam has a social purpose, which is to dissuade others from committing the same crime. People nowadays, especially Westerners, are opposed to the Islamic punishment for fornication and adultery because they see it as too harsh or disproportionate to the offense. A basic problem is the difference in standards by which the severity of a crime is measured.

The Western view of man-woman relationships is usually that of permissiveness, one that accepts extramarital and illicit relationships as normal. There is an increasingly driving passion for more money, more comforts and more pleasure, particularly physical pleasure. The greatest casualty of irresponsible sexual behavior has been the family, in particular, children.

Islam views sexual relationships outside of marriage as a very serious matter because they destabilize the family and thus contribute to the breakdown of the entire social system. Islam emphasizes protection of the family by imposing severe punishments for activities that threaten the family foundation. These punishments are the same for men and women and only a legitimate Islamic government has the right to implement them.

Moreover, the prescribed punishments are only one aspect of a complete system which, in addition to providing prohibitive obstacles in the path of unlawful relationships, strongly encourages and facilitates lawful marriage. In cases of confirmed incompatibility or dissatisfaction, a wife as well as a husband may request separation, enabling each to seek a more harmonious union. In addition, Muslims, whether married or unmarried, are instructed as to proper dress and behavior at all times. Privacy is to be respected and compromising situations strictly avoided as a matter of obedience to God. And finally, the punishment prescribed is severe enough to deter any who might still consider it.

Any case that comes before the court for judgment must be investigated thoroughly and proper evidence brought in order to satisfy all the requirements of Islamic law. Conviction is subject to strict conditions which are most difficult to fulfill and is contingent on one of two requirements:

· A repeated and persistent confession by the offender, who must also be proved to be of age, mentally sound, aware of the divine prohibition, and must have committed the act knowingly of his own free will. The slightest doubt about any of these matters will prevent acceptance of the confession. In addition, a married adulterer must be legally bound in a consummated marriage and there must be no physical defect in the spouse preventing a normal relationship. Furthermore, people are not encouraged to confess their sins; rather, they should repent to God privately.

- In the absence of confession there can be no conviction unless four reliable male Muslim witnesses known for honesty and righteous conduct testify that they actually saw the act taking place. It is insufficient that the couple was seen together, even if undressed and in an embrace. Witnesses must be unanimous about the time, place and other details; otherwise, the case will be rejected. This means that in reality the punishment is seldom carried out and serves primarily as a deterrent. As an additional precaution, anyone who makes such an accusation outside the framework of these conditions is himself subject to a severe punishment.

Any government under which Shari'ah legislation is applied must establish justice as its core value in all affairs so that the social and cultural environment is suitable for all its people to live an upright and moral life. It is only after these conditions have been fulfilled that a government is entitled to implement penalties on its land.

31. Why is a woman's share of inheritance half that of a man?

The Islamic system of property distribution after death is based on rulings ordained by God in the Qur'an. It abolished the former custom in which the entire estate was taken by the oldest male heir and established the right of children, parents and spouses to inherit a specific share without leaving the matter to human judgement and emotion. When Islam established inheritance for the woman, it was the first time in history that women were able to enjoy this right. The Qur'an stipulates that a woman automatically inherits from her father, husband, son and her childless brother.

This system of inheritance is perfectly balanced and is based on the closeness of relationship, also taking into account the responsibilities imposed upon various members of a family in different situations. In the absence of close relatives a share is apportioned to more distant ones.

When the male is given a larger share there is a logical reason behind it, which is that in Islam economic responsibility is always upon the man while the woman has no financial obligations even if she should be wealthy or have her own income. Generally, the woman is in charge of running the household and taking care of those within it, so she is justly freed from financial responsibilities. When unmarried it is the legal obligation of her father, brother or guardian to provide her food, clothing, medication, housing and other needs. After marriage it becomes the duty of her husband or adult son. Islam holds men responsible by law for fulfilling all the needs of their families. So the difference in shares does not in any way mean that one sex is preferred over the other. Rather, it represents a just balance consistent with the needs and responsibilities of family members.

When a son and a daughter inherit from either of their parents, the son's share will be depleted by giving an obligatory dowry to his wife upon marriage and maintaining his family, including his sister until she marries. While the daughter has no required expenses, she still receives a share of the inheritance which is her own property to save, invest or use as she pleases. When she marries she will also receive a dowry from her husband and be maintained by him, having no financial responsibilities whatsoever. Thus, one might conclude that Islam has favored women over men!

Although in most cases the male inherits a share that is twice that of a female, it is not always so. There are certain circumstances when they inherit equal shares, and in a few instances a female can inherit a larger share than that of the male.

In addition, a Muslim can will up to one third of his property by bequest to anyone who would not inherit from him by law. The bequest may be a means of assistance to other relatives and people who are in need, whether men or women. One may also allocate this portion or part of it to charities and good works of his choice.

32. Why is the testimony of two women required in place of one man?

What is meant by testimony is: giving information by which something is known to be true and correct. With regard to the witness of two women being equal to the testimony of one man, it is not always the case, but the Qur'anic verse that specifies this is related only to financial dealings, where two men are preferred and the alternative is one man and two women. Financial transactions constitute the sole case in which two female witnesses are required in place of one male witness. It is in view of the fact that financial responsibility is usually shouldered by men so they are expected to be better versed in financial transactions than women. It also takes into account the more emotional nature of women generally as well as the roles of men and women in society as envisaged by Islam.

This does not reflect inferiority on the woman's part. Some women surpass most men in many aspects, including religious commitment, reasoning and memory. They may have a great deal of interest in certain matters and thus able to give proper testimony better than that of a man regarding the issues in which they have knowledge and insight. They can even become references regarding them as did some women at the time of the Prophet. A judge may accept the testimony of any person of exceptional qualifications.

Two female witnesses are not always considered equal to one male witness. There are other verses in the Qur'an which speak about witnesses without specifying male or female. In those cases, a female witness is equivalent to a male witness. It is well known that Aisha, the Prophet's wife, related no less than 2220 narrations which are considered authentic only on her solitary evidence. Other women have also been recognized as reliable narrators of prophetic traditions. This is sufficient proof that the witness of one women can be accepted.

In fact, female witnesses are preferred in certain cases. There are incidents which require only female witnesses and the testimony of a male is not accepted. Issues pertaining to women alone such as childbirth or menstruation as related to divorce disputes and private matters where no men were present obviously necessitate the witness of a woman.

Social and Family Issues

33. Isn't Islam intolerant of other religions? How should Muslims treat people of other faiths?

Tolerance is the attitude that should govern the dealings of all people with one another. Religious tolerance is an essential principle of Islam and Muslims are ordered to have good relations with people of all religions and be kind and courteous to everyone. Muslims are ordered by the Qur'an to uphold their covenants with the non-Muslims and not betray them or transgress against them. The lives, families, properties and honor of non-Muslims must be protected under any government that claims to apply Islamic law. Non-Muslims are also guaranteed the right and freedom to practice their own religions in an Islamic state.

Islam is a religion of mercy and justice. It teaches its adherents to interact with all people and to cooperate with them for the betterment of mankind. More than ever today, Muslims need to work together with other groups that oppose oppression, bloodshed, corruption, promiscuity and perversion. They should also cooperate with non-Muslims in upholding truth and combating falsehood, in supporting the oppressed and eliminating such dangers as pollution and disease.

Only enemies who harbor hatred and contempt against Islam are addressed by those Qur'anic verses that warn Muslims against taking them as intimates and allies. Muslims are ordered to deal with all other human beings with justice and compassion as members of the human brotherhood. They are always to behave kindly toward any non-Muslims who are not hostile, whether by offering financial help, feeding the hungry, giving loans when needed or interceding in connection with permissible matters, even by speaking kindly and advising them. The Qur'an addresses believers, saying:

"Allah does not forbid you from those who do not fight you because of religion and do not expel you from your homes, from being righteous toward them acting justly toward them. Indeed, Allah loves those who are just." [50]

Thus, it is not permissible under any circumstance for Muslims to mistreat a non-Muslim who has not committed any aggression against them; they not allowed to harm,

---

[50] 60:8.

threaten or terrorize him, steal his wealth, cheat him or deprive him of his rights. It is obligatory upon Muslims as well to honor whatever lawful treaties and agreements are made with non-Muslim parties.

Coexistence does not mean that we cease to promote our positive values. As an aspect of their kindness and concern for humanity, Muslims are expected to invite non-Muslims to the truth of Islam with words of wisdom, sound arguments and a pleasant manner. This is a debt owed by Muslims to the peoples of the world in gratitude to God for His guidance and countless blessings.

34. What is Islam's attitude toward Western civilization today?

Humanity lives crowded together in an increasingly small world of various cultures. Undoubtedly, Western culture is the dominant influence in the modern world today. Hence, it is inevitable that others interact with it and assimilate its positive values and achievements, but without adopting its negative ones. There is a cultural dimension of most human phenomena, religion included, and modern societies are tending to become less exclusive and more multi-religious. But while people are developing an outlook that is more accommodating toward others, acknowledging these differences does not mean that there should be no distinction between good and evil.

As well as being a religion and way of life, Islam is also a complete worldview. Its attitude toward the present western civilization is the same as that manifested toward every past civilization: it accepts the goodness that such civilizations can yield but at the same time rejects their evils. It allows for the acquisition of particular benefits such as scientific and technical knowledge, yet many social aspects are seen to be destructive and contrary to Islamic teachings.

Islam has never advocated a policy of isolationism. It does not oppose other civilizations merely because they are non-Muslim, but believes in the unity of humanity and good relationships with people of different races and inclinations. And Muslims do not object to benefiting from modernity in discovering the mechanisms for solving common problems or to the solutions themselves, as long as they do not contradict Islamic legislation.

Islam neither rejects the West totally nor does it accept it uncritically. Led by political and economic interests, the upholders of Western civilization often follow policies which are detrimental to the collective good of Muslims. What Muslims and many other peoples of the world today reject is the presumed centrality and universalism of the West and its self-centered attitude. They opposed the oppression and exploitation perpetrated by Western colonialism in the past, and they object to the newer, albeit more subtle forms, which are no less malevolent. Injustices caused by arrogant attitudes and policies are unacceptable to everyone.

Opening up to the modern worldview and critically interacting with it has alerted Muslims to certain problems raised by Western modernity. International relations, globalization, the menace posed by the media and central government to the human individual, the increase of leisure time available to ordinary people and the processes of standardization were issues seldom raised in the past. The study of Western modernity in a critical and interactive manner may serve to sharpen the awareness of Muslims concerning the magnitude of the global culture crisis and consequently, increase their knowledge and confidence in their own divinely ordained way of life.

It can be fairly said that Islam does not oppose any civilization as long as it serves the interests of humanity. But customs of other cultures involving principles or conduct prohibited in Islam can never be considered as lawful for a Muslim, even one who resides permanently in non-Muslim lands. The limits set by God are protective ones which must always be observed, and Islam stands firm to uphold this right for mankind.

35. Why is so much of the Muslim world underdeveloped?

No one can deny that the Muslim world has been in decline for several centuries, the causes of which go back into history. In the Muslim nation's early stages, wealth, centers of learning and public works were abundant. But affluence, excessive concern with worldly life and the spread of corruption eventually weakened religious consciousness. The inevitable result of these human failures was an ebb in conversions to Islam and territorial expansion, losses sustained in East Asia and Europe, the ascension of Western power and influence and a change from an ascendant to a defensive posture. The present backwardness of most Muslim societies, their political degradation and their peoples' suffering, in spite of their human and material resources and of Islam's noble values and principles, is the unfortunate reality of the present day.

The calamities that befell the Muslim world after the period of its early expansion, eventually leading to the fall of the caliphate, cannot be attributed to Islamic thought or even entirely to errors in political leadership. The prophetic period and that of the early caliphs which followed presented the best examples for all succeeding generations.

However, the rapid influx of new peoples and nations into the community of Islam before they were properly educated as to Islamic objectives and values resulted in a later political leadership that never developed and matured as it should have. The Islamic vision became obscured and its spirit reduced to mere form, empty words and a heritage venerated, but seriously misunderstood, by later generations. The natural trend of Islamic legal system to expand was arrested and the vital physical sciences, economics, sociology and political thought – all essential aspects of previous development – were neglected. At the same time the Muslim world was becoming increasingly weak and vulnerable, Europe was beginning to benefit from the achievements of Islamic scholarship and assert itself.

The fact that most Muslim regions of the world were then conquered, dominated and exploited by Western colonial powers for some time is not an excuse that is condoned by Islam. Rather, it was the natural outcome of the widespread neglect and failure by Muslims to conscientiously and comprehensively adhere to the teachings of their religion.

The importance of obtaining knowledge and working conscientiously with determination was made clear by the Prophet of Islam. Muslims are taught that because man has been given a certain amount of free will it must be exercised properly in accordance with Islamic teachings to earn approval of the Creator. This in itself is motivation for Muslims to be the most knowledgeable and productive people possible. If Muslim societies today are not meeting their potential, it is surely not due to Islam; rather it is from their ignorance of the religion and failure to apply and practice it.

36. If Islam is such a good religion, why do we find many Muslims dishonest, unreliable and lazy?

Islam came as a message of guidance from God to all creation at a time when ignorance and corruption were universal. It opened peoples' minds and souls to learning, development, refinement and morality. The achievements of Islamic thought in that early period were sufficient to bring light, guidance and knowledge to humanity.

However, as among every other people, there are indeed some Muslims who are heedless, undependable, corrupt and selfish, and the media projects this stereotype about Muslims in particular. It can be readily noted that whenever an adherent to any other faith commits a crime, the media seldom brings up the issue of religion, but when a Muslim is involved, it is Islam that is blamed and portrayed in a negative light before public opinion.

The fact cannot be denied that many Muslims today are unmindful of the teachings of their religion, due either to a lack of religious knowledge or to various worldly inducements and attractions. But even if one recognizes that some Muslims may be dishonest, immoral or impulsive, he should not judge Islam by its nonconforming or disobedient members, but rather by those who conscientiously adhere to its teachings. Since Islam categorically forbids such evils as lying, cheating and negligence, the wrongdoer must be blamed for his crimes rather than the religion. One should instead examine the system itself, understand its principles and disregard the acts of those who have serious deficiencies in their knowledge, beliefs and practice.

While today's Muslim societies are not model ones by any means, they still enjoy a comparatively stable family life, absence of delinquency, low crime rates, greater freedom from drugs and alcoholism, as well as the warmth of brotherhood, generosity and mutual aid. It may be observed that taken as a whole, the Muslim community produces the best citizens in any society. As a matter of religious observance, the majority avoids the consumption of alcohol and drugs, eliminating many intoxicant-related crimes. Collectively, Muslims are the community which gives the maximum amount of charity in the world. And no community can equal Muslims where modesty, sobriety and human ethics are concerned.

Islam may be fairly and justly assessed not by negative stereotypes portrayed by the media, but by what its authentic sources contain and by the practice of the most excellent follower of the religion, Prophet Muhammad. There have been a number of unbiased non-Muslim historians who have declared that Muhammad was an exemplary human being. It is his pattern of life that demonstrates the true Islamic ideal and example to be followed by Muslims.

37. What is Islam's view about education, science and technology?

The framework of Islamic thought represents a comprehensive view of life and the universe. A Muslim is required to acquire both religious and worldly knowledge. In fact, Islam advocated knowledge at a time when the whole world was engulfed in ignorance. In a matter of years, the early generation of Muslims became a learned and refined people, for Islam had awakened in them the faculty of intellect. Those early Muslims understood from the teachings of their religion that useful knowledge is necessary for the benefit of the self and of humanity. Hence, they pursued it to such a degree that they surpassed other nations in development and productivity and carried the torch of civilization for many centuries.

Muslim history abounds with examples of scientific and cultural ingenuity. Muslims inherited the knowledge of the nations that came before them, developed it and placed it in the context of a precise moral framework. Muslim scholarship made a vital contribution to the enrichment and advancement of human civilization.

While Europe was still in the dark ages, religious Muslims were making great advances in the fields of medicine, mathematics, physics, astronomy, geography, architecture, literature, and history documentation to mention but a few. Many important new procedures such as the use of algebra, Arabic numerals with the principle of the zero, vital to the advancement of mathematics, were transmitted to medieval Europe from Muslim regions. Sophisticated instruments, such as the astrolabe and the quadrant, as well as good navigational maps, were first developed by Muslims. Only after people lost sight of their religious beliefs and obligations did the scientific achievements of the Muslim world cease and fall into obscurity.

Similarly, Islam does not now oppose any modern inventions that are beneficial to mankind. It is sufficient that they be used in the name of God and for His cause. In reality, machines, instruments and devices have no religion or homeland. They can be used for either good or bad objectives, and the way they are used can affect much of the earth's population. Even something so simple as a glass can be filled either with a nourishing drink or with a poison. Television can provide education or immorality. It is up to the user to decide, and a Muslim is commanded to make good use of all the means at his disposal while being prohibited from causing harm to himself or others. Failure to use the proper means toward benefit is, in effect, a deprecation of Islamic teachings.

A truly Islamic government is required to the best of its ability to provide all means that promote adequate education for its citizens. Education is a right for all individuals and the required moral duty of every capable Muslim. All able, intelligent and skilled individuals in an Islamic society are required to educate themselves not only in the basics of their religion but in necessary worldly affairs. Further, it is obligatory upon qualified people to study every beneficial field of knowledge. For example, since every society needs doctors, it becomes obligatory for some people to go into the field of medicine to fulfill the needs of society.

Advancements in science and technology are among the ways and means to achieve development of the Muslim world. Islam calls upon Muslims to pursue knowledge in the broadest sense of the word. Prophet Muhammad said, "Seeking knowledge is an obligation upon every Muslim."[51] He also said, "For one who treads a path to knowledge, Allah will make easy the path to Paradise."[52] And the Qur'an contains numerous references to knowledge and its importance, such as:

> *Indeed, in the creation of the heavens and the earth and the alternation of night and day are signs for those of understanding.[53]*
>
> *Say: "Are those who know equal to those who do not know?"[54]*
>
> *Allah will raise those who have believed among you and those who were given knowledge by degrees.[55]*

Qur'anic verses encourage study and contemplation of the universe that surrounds us and is particularly concerned with those sciences that give human beings the ability to benefit from the world around them. While encouraging investigation, the Qur'an contains references to a variety of subjects which have

---

[51] Narrated by Ibn Majah.
[52] Narrated by Muslim.
[53] 3:190.
[54] 39:9.
[55] 58:11.

been shown to be scientifically accurate.[56] This is the fulfillment of God's statement over 14 centuries ago:

> *"We will show them Our signs in the horizons and within themselves until it becomes clear to them that it is the truth."[57]*

Thus, when a Muslim has a sincere and wholesome intention to obtain knowledge, it will also have a positive effect on his faith. For knowledge reinforces textual evidence for the existence of the almighty Creator and assists in appreciation of the many scientific allusions found in the Qur'an.

There has never been an established scientific fact that contradicted the teachings of Islam. Whatever modern science discovers only increases the Muslim's knowledge of God's magnificent creation. Thus, Islam actively encourages scientific endeavors and the study of God's signs in nature. It also welcomes beneficial technological advances and allows people to enjoy the fruits of human ingenuity.

To a Muslim, conflict between science and religion is an impossibility, for religion comes from God and so does His system of creation and development. The modern, purely materialistic approach to scientific and technological advancement has indeed granted man a measure of physical comfort, but not mental or spiritual comfort. Islam advocates the incorporation of knowledge within a just and balanced value system where anything beneficial for one's spiritual and worldly improvement is encouraged and advocated.

38. Does Islam accept slavery?

Sometimes people ask why Islam did not abolish slavery. They tend to forget that other religions did not do

---

[56] A few such examples were cited on p.32-33.
[57] 41:53.

so either; in fact, there are several passages in the Bible that order slaves to serve their masters well. It is well known that when Europe made contact with Africa, the black people of that continent were faced with a major calamity of human misery that lasted more than five centuries. Slavery was not abolished worldwide until the year 1953, through a resolution issued by the United Nations.

At the time of the Qur'an's revelation, slavery was a universal institution upon which the economies of every civilization were dependent. There were many ways by which a slave could be obtained, such as poverty (forcing one to sell himself or his children into slavery), debt (when a debtor could not pay off his debt, he became a slave), kidnapping and raids. Islam limited the sources that existed previously to one: the capture of enemy prisoners during war; and all others were prohibited.

Actually, Islam is unique in its concern for the peaceful elimination of this practice. Due to His perfect knowledge and wisdom, God did not order slavery abolished outright. Since the economy of every civilization on earth was based and dependent upon this system, not only would the Muslim community have been put at great disadvantage by the immediate emancipation of all slaves, but the slaves themselves would have been unprepared for release into society without homes or means of support.

Mercifully, God made the freeing of slaves within Islam a gradual transition. Manumission by the state and by individual Muslims was encouraged as a righteous deed greatly rewarded in the Hereafter. The Qur'an stated that obligatory zakah and charity funds could be used for the purchase of slaves to be freed, and freeing a slave is cited therein as expiation for breaking an oath and for the commission of particular kinds of sins and errors. Moreover, a good slave could enter into a contract with his master to earn his freedom. Thousands of slaves requested and were granted contracts of emancipation by their Muslim owners.

Prophet Muhammad repeatedly emphasized good treatment of the slaves who remained, severely rebuking those owners who transgressed. Under Islam slaves were to be given the same quality of food and clothing as their masters, they were not to be overworked, their dignity was to be preserved and they were to be treated with justice and kindness. Often, slaves became members of Muslim families and refused freedom. Only under Islam did the slave enjoy a unique position as a member of the household and community worthy of respect.

In many cases, a slave would become a close friend and advisor of his master; or the master would even regard him as a son. It was not uncommon for slaves to be given precedence over free men regarding religious or worldly matters in which one of them excelled. For example, a slave well versed in the Qur'an could lead the prayer, and Muslims were ordered to obey if a slave should be appointed in charge of their affairs.

Islam has always encouraged the emancipation of slaves with the objective of gradually diminishing their numbers and integrating them into society. As a result of Islamic teachings, slavery was almost completely eradicated from many areas of the Muslim world, peacefully and without bloodshed. Can any other religion or civilization make such a claim?

39. Is there any mention of human rights in Islam?

Islam has laid down universal and fundamental rights for humanity as a whole, which are to be observed and respected under all circumstances. These basic rights are associated with Islamic faith and belief because they are divinely ordained. Thus, human rights in Islam are religious obligations, meaning that it is obligatory for every Muslim to protect them and restore them if they are violated.

Islam declares all people equal in terms of human values, and all individuals are equal before the Islamic code of law. Its judgments and legal penalties are applicable to all races and classes of people without any distinction and without any person, group or nation acquiring immunity or privilege. Every human being is entitled to his integrity, honor and reputation during his life and after his death.

Islam condemns the abuse of power, position and authority and commands people to assist an oppressed person even with the use of force when necessary. Every individual in an Islamic society, regardless of his faith or religious affiliation, position or social status, has certain immutable rights, which include:

- The right to be consulted on issues that concern their economic and social affairs
- The right to be considered innocent unless proven guilty
- The right to seek judgment against oppressors and to have an equal hearing before the judge

It is an unfortunate reality of our time, however, that the governments of many so-called 'Muslim' countries today do not apply these principles, but rather suppress public opinion and violate human rights. However, such tyranny is in no way representative of Islamic teachings. In fact, the Prophet of Islam warned, "The most ruthless in punishing people in this world will be the most ruthlessly punished of people by God on the Day of Resurrection."[58] And the Qur'an clearly commands:

---

[58] Narrated by Ahmad - saheeh.

"O you who have believed, stand up firmly for God and witness with justice, and do not let hatred of a people prevent you from being just. Be just; that is nearer to righteousness."[59]

No one may be arrested, exiled, punished or his freedom restricted without adequate legal action. No one may be subjected to physical or psychological torment, medical experimentation or any other humiliating treatment. And it is not permitted to empower executive authority to issue exceptional laws.

These human rights are comprehensive and applicable to every person under Islamic jurisdiction, regardless of his race, religion, nationality or social status. They cannot be altered at any time or under any circumstance. Violation of these rights is a violation against the divine decree and necessitates punishment in the Hereafter in addition to that of this world, unless the offender repents and reforms.

If such human rights had never been enforced at some time in human history they would have remained no more than theoretical ideals in people's minds. But Prophet Muhammad founded a civilization in which they were fully implemented, serving as an outstanding example for all future generations of mankind.

A Muslim believer is obligated to oppose injustice and oppression no matter who the victim happens to be. When seeing another human being in distress or critical need of assistance, it is his duty to help that person; otherwise, he is accountable for whatever increase in suffering was caused by his neglect. Even during war it is not permissible to harm women, children, the elderly, the sick or the wounded. The hungry person must be fed, the naked clothed, and the

---

[59] 5:8.

wounded or diseased treated medically, irrespective of who they are.

Under Islam the lives and properties of all citizens are inviolable, whether they are Muslims or not. The right of security and protection to a person and his family is the most basic of all rights. It is unlawful in a Muslim society for any of its citizens to be harassed or threatened by words, acts or weapons of any type. For the protection of human life in particular, Islam has required severe punishments for criminals who murder, injure and harm others.

One of the fundamental rights established by the sacred texts is that no one can be compelled to accept Islam. It is the duty of Muslims to establish the proofs of Islam to people so that truth can be distinguished from falsehood. After that, whoever wishes to accept Islam may do so and whoever wishes to continue in unbelief may do so.

40. Doesn't Islam oppress women?

Many people think of Islam as a chauvinistic religion that demeans women, and the stereotype image of the completely secluded and oppressed Muslim woman is all too common. They cite the condition of women in some Muslim countries to emphasize the point, but their error is that they fail to make a distinction between the practices of those people and the true teachings of the religion that they profess.

Although women have been oppressed by Muslims in some cultures, this should not be understood as coming from the religion, but rather, it reflects customs that are inconsistent, if not completely contrary to Islamic teachings. And it is true that some Muslim men still oppress women today; but then, so do many non-Muslim men. When Muslims are at fault it is either because of cultural habit or their ignorance about Islam. In actual fact, Islam expects its adherents to uphold the rights of women, protect their social status and prevent their degradation in any way.

The status of women in earlier civilizations was so low that they were denied basic human dignity. Prostitution was a regular practice, and many considered women to be basically evil, subhuman and inferior to men. Before Islam, the Arabs disdained women, and often when a female child was born she was buried alive. Islam uplifted women and gave them honor and equal status; and it requires that this status be upheld and maintained.

Islam secured for the woman her intellectual, religious, social, economic and political rights, including the right to an education, the right to own property and to use it at her own discretion, and the right to work. A Muslim woman is a completely independent personality. In addition to her right to think and believe as she likes, Islam considers her to be an active member of society who can make a valuable contribution. From the dawn of Islam, women engaged in many occupations such as commerce, agriculture, and manufacturing. A Muslim woman can make any contract or bequest in her own name. She is entitled to inherit in her position as mother, a wife, a sister and a daughter. It is not permissible for anyone to take a woman's wealth without her consent. And there is consensus among the scholars of Islam that all economic activities of a woman, like buying, selling, leasing, giving gifts, and giving collateral, are legally valid and that she has a completely independent economic existence.

Women have the right to a decent life, without facing aggression or being wronged. Women have the right to be educated, to express themselves, to give sincere advice, to enjoin what is good and forbid what is evil, and to invite people to Islam. None of these basic principles have changed, but regarding their application, there can be no doubt that the weaker religious commitment has grown among Muslims, the more these rights have been neglected.

Modern Western societies claim to have improved the condition of women but have actually demoted them to the level of slaves in the hands of pleasure seekers and sex marketers by convincing them that they should be freed from religious and social restrictions. The United States of America is one of the leading advocates of women's "liberation," but it also has one of the highest rates of rape and sexual harassment in the world. A woman's proclaimed right to seek employment and climb the ladder of success is seldom without compromise. But much is overlooked in the quest to be "equal" with men.

As a fundamental principle, Islam holds that women are indeed equal to men in their origin, their humanity, their honor and their accountability before God. They are also equal in their need to fulfill their physical and material needs, to possess property and dispose of it as they wish. Both sexes are required to obtain knowledge; in fact, it is the religious duty of every Muslim man and woman. Women used to seek knowledge at the mosque and in the home of Prophet Muhammad. They even asked him to set aside a day for teaching them, and he did so. There were many excellent scholars, jurists and writers among women during the era of the Prophet's companions and their students, as well as in later periods of Islamic history.

The notion that Islam makes women second class citizens worth half a man is no more than a myth. Over 1,400 years ago Islam elevated the status of women by declaring them sisters of men, giving them the right of education to the highest level, the right to choose a husband, the right to end an unhappy marriage, the right to inheritance and in general, the rights of a full citizen of the state.

Under Islamic law it is unlawful for a woman to be married off without her consent or forced into a marriage. She has the right to initiate a separation from marriage if her rights are not being granted or she cannot bear the husband. Prophet Muhammad is known to have annulled marriages of women who had been unwillingly coerced. Widows and divorcees have the right to remarry and are in fact encouraged to do so. When a Muslim woman marries she does not give up her family name and keeps her distinct identity.

In Muslim marriages the husband is required to give a dowry to his wife which becomes her private property and is not subject to the dictates of her male relatives. Similarly, any money she earns or receives, whether she is married or not, is her own to use in any way she sees fit. Islam places on men the obligation of protecting and maintaining all of their female relatives, and a man must provide for his wife even if she has money of her own. She is not obligated to spend anything in maintenance of her family, and is thus relieved of the need to seek employment. However, she may work if she prefers to or if circumstances warrant it.

The family, like any other organization, requires order and leadership. The Qur'an has given the husband a "degree" of authority over the wife, which means responsibility, guardianship and accountability. It is in no way a license to practice tyranny within the household; rather, it is the burden of responsibility to care completely and conscientiously for one's wife and children. In turn, obedience is due to him, but only pertaining to what is right and fair according to the Islamic Shari'ah. The Qur'an states:

And due to [women] is what is similar to that expected from them.[60]

Not only are material and physical rights specified, but those of kindness and consideration are equally significant in Islamic law.

41. Are men and women considered equal?

When replying to this question, we must first define what is meant by "equal" and identify the aspect which worries us in terms of gender equality. Islam regards women as spiritual and intellectual equals of men. For a Muslim, the important issue is who can become closest to God and earn the greatest reward. The Qur'an answers:

Whoever does deeds of righteousness, whether male or female, while being a believer – those will enter Paradise, and not the least injustice will be done to them.[61]

For Muslim men and women, for believing men and women, for devout men and women, for truthful men and women, for patient men and women, for humble men and women, for charitable men and women, for fasting men and women, for chaste men and women, and for men and women who remember God often – for them has Allah prepared forgiveness and great reward.[62]

There is no difference between men and women as far as their relationship to God is concerned. Both are equal before

---

[60] 2:228.
[61] 4:124.
[62] 33:35.

God[63] and they are both accountable before Him. Women, like men, are commanded to worship God and both are promised the same rewards and punishments according to their intention and conduct.

Economically, every man and woman is an independent legal entity. Both men and women have the right to own property, engage in business, and inherit from others. Both have the equal right to receive an education and enter into gainful employment. Seeking knowledge is an obligation upon every Muslim, and to prevent women from getting an education is contrary to the teachings of Islam.

However, one fact mentioned in the Qur'an and now recognized is that all things are created in pairs. Had there been a similar function for all, the creation of two counterparts would not have been necessary. To ignore inherent physical and psychological differences is surely unrealistic, but there is no reason to assume that one sex is superior to the other. The creation of male and female means a natural division of function, meaning distinct roles for each, which are both complementary and collaborative.

Thus, absolute equality between men and women in all matters is neither possible nor reasonable. But this does not mean bias in favor of men to the detriment of women. While some rulings may be seen to favor men, many others favor women. However, most Islamic rulings apply to men and women equally, and both are bound by their obligations towards one another. The main distinction between the two sexes is in the physical realm, based on the equitable principle of fair division of labor. Islam allots the more strenuous work to the man and makes him responsible for

---

[63] God is neither male nor female. Gender is an attribute of creation but not the Creator. The use of the pronoun "He" for God is a linguistic one, used in the Qur'an and accepted by Muslims as such.

the maintenance of the family. It allots the work of managing the home and the upbringing and training of children to the woman, work which has the greatest importance in the task of building a healthy and prosperous society.

It is also true that sound administration within any organization requires a unified policy under a just executive. For this reason Islam expects the husband, as head of the household, to consult with his family and then have the final say in decisions concerning it. This degree of authority in no way means that the Creator prefers men over women but is simply the logical way of apportioning responsibilities in a household. Men and women are two equally important component parts of humanity, and the rights and responsibilities of both sexes in Islam are equitable and balanced in their totality. Although their obligations might differ in certain areas of life in accordance with basic physical and psychological differences, each one is equally accountable for his or her particular responsibilities.

42. Why does Islam keep women behind the veil?

The Islamic veil or "hijab" refers to the loose-fitting, opaque outer garments with which a Muslim woman covers her head and body.[64] Muslim women cover themselves with such garments before all men apart from their closest relatives. They do not do so to please their fathers, brothers or husbands, but only because God has ordained it. In reality, Islam did not introduce modest dress but merely endorsed it as part of God's religion. Yet, dress is only one aspect of a total concept.

---

[64] While basically the same as the clothing depicted in traditional Christian representations of the Virgin Mary, this type of dress is currently singled out as sign of Islamic extremism.

"Hijab" is not merely a concealing garment but includes proper behavior, manners, speech and appearance in public.

In order to accept any law or instruction, a person needs either to be convinced of the benefit behind it or to trust in the wisdom of the one who prescribed it. Muslims believe that the wisdom of God is absolute and perfect and that He knows the nature and best interests of His creations (mankind included) better than they do themselves; thus, a believer willingly obeys God's directives as much as he or she is able.

To some, the matter of women's dress might seem trivial. Islam, however, assigns to it moral, social and legal dimensions. When women observe the proper Islamic dress, they protect their own honor and reputation and contribute greatly towards peace and order in society.

Modesty is a virtue which Islam demands of both men and women, not only for the protection of women, but to maintain the spiritual uprightness of men. In view of the sexual anarchy that prevails in many parts of the world, the need for modest dress and behavior in both men and women is obvious. However, on account of differences between males and females in nature and temperament, a greater amount of privacy is required for women than for men, and this relates, among other things, to their manner of dress.

Islam has no fixed standard as to the style of dress or type of clothing that must be worn. However, it must be wide and thick enough as not to reveal the contours of the figure. Muslim women are responsible for making their homes attractive and comfortable, and Islam encourages a woman to beautify herself for her husband and immediate family members rather than exhibiting her physical charms and worldly possessions publicly.

Muslim women who cover themselves do not find it impractical or interfering with their activities in the various fields of life. It is often forgotten that the modern Western style of dress is a recent phenomenon. Looking at the clothing of women as recently as seventy years ago, we see that it is similar to the dress prescribed by Islam. Those hard-working, active Western women were not at all inhibited by their long, full dresses and head coverings.

The covering of women's bodies is not a logical basis on which to claim that women are subservient to men. It would be far more appropriate to charge a society with exploitation of females when it tolerates pornography rather than when it encourages modesty. It is ironic that uncontested freedom is granted to those who choose to publicly expose much of their bodies, while severe censure is launched against women who consider that modest covering is a religious obligation that cannot be disregarded.

Islam teaches that women are to be evaluated for their intelligence, opinions, skills, deeds and inner qualities rather than physical appearance. A Muslim woman who covers her body is making a statement about herself and her identity; she has dignity, respectability, self esteem and is proud of her Islam. Whoever sees her will know that she is not available to men or interested in advances, that she has an upright moral character and that she will not permit sexuality to enter into any of her necessary interactions with the opposite sex. Women often see their Islamic dress as empowering because they are taken seriously and respected rather than being viewed as sex objects; they are judged only by their character and conduct.

43. Why is a Muslim man allowed to have more than one wife?

Although it is found in many religious and cultural traditions, polygamy is most often identified with Islam in the minds of Westerners.

However, one does not find any limit to the number of wives in the Talmud, Bible, Hindu scriptures or others. Therefore, polygamy is not something exclusive to Islam. There was no restriction on Hindu men regarding the number of wives until 1954, when Indian civil law made it illegal for a non-Muslim to have more than one wife. It continued among the Jewish Sephardic communities until as late as 1950, when an Act of the Chief Rabbinate of Israel declared it unlawful to marry more than one wife. And Christian men were originally permitted to take as many wives as they wished since the Bible placed no limit on the number. It was only in recent centuries that the Church limited the number of wives to one. Unrestricted polygamy has been practiced in most human societies throughout the world until fairly recently.

In a world which allowed men an unlimited number of wives, it was Islam which limited the number to four. Before the Qur'an was revealed, there was no upper limit and many men had scores of wives, some into the hundreds. Islam placed the limit at four and gave a man permission to marry two, three or four on the condition that he must deal with all of them benevolently and fairly, as indicated in the Qur'an:

But if you fear that you will not be just, then [marry] only one. [65]

The Qur'an is the only religious book that says, "marry only one." The idea that it is compulsory for a Muslim man to have more than one wife is a misconception. Polygamy

---

[65] 4:3.

falls into the category of things that are permissible but not obligatory. Taking an additional wife is neither encouraged nor prohibited. Islam allows a man to marry up to four wives provided he can support them all adequately and treat each one fairly. Just and fair treatment involves what is within the husband's ability, such as the time spent with each, expenditures, gifts, etc.[66] If he knows or even fears that he will be unable to do so, it is not permissible for him to marry more than one wife. This Qur'anic directive strengthens the position of the family and of women, for it provides legal security for many women who would otherwise remain unmarried.

It is a known fact that the world female population is now more than the male population. Infant mortality rates among males are higher when compared to that of females. During wars, more men are killed as compared to women. More men die due to accidents and diseases than women. The average life span of females is longer than that of males. Thus, at almost any given time and place, there is a shortage of men in comparison to women. And when men are taken out of the marriage market by wars or economic difficulties it is women who suffer.

What are women of honor and self respect to do is such situations? How can they fulfill their natural desire to have companionship and sexual relations without resorting to fornication, adultery, lesbianism or other perverted practices? The only options open to unmarried women are to remain deprived of a relationship for the rest of their lives, to become "public property" or to marry a married man. Islam prefers giving women the advantage by

---

[66] Love and physical attraction are matters of the heart, usually beyond a man's ability to control; therefore, those differences are excused. Not excused, however, is an obvious display of favor or aversion toward one in particular, or injustice in terms of their marital rights. Equal treatment of each remains a strict condition.

permitting and facilitating legal marriage and prohibiting irresponsible relationships.

The Western insistence on monogamy is essentially false. In their societies today it is not uncommon for a man to have extramarital relations with girlfriends, mistresses or prostitutes. Seldom is this disapproved of despite the harm that comes about from it. Soaring divorce rates, broken homes, deadbeat dads, increasing numbers of children born out of wedlock and the spread of sexually transmitted diseases are just a few of the negative consequences of this common practice. Additionally, the woman in such a relationship has no legal rights. She will easily be cast aside to fend for herself should she become pregnant or when the man simply tires of her.

Within marriage the woman has a husband who is obligated by law to provide for her and her children. There is no doubt that a second wife lawfully married and treated honorably is better off than a mistress without any legal rights or social respect. Islam has allowed more than one wife in order to protect society from immorality and to uphold the honor and dignity of women.

Polygamy protects the interests of women and children within society and also prevents the spread of venereal diseases, herpes and AIDS, which are rampant in promiscuous societies where extra-marital affairs abound. After World War II, when suggestions to legalize polygamy were rejected by the Church in Germany, prostitution was legalized instead. The rate of marriage has been steadily declining there as the new generation finds marriage increasingly unnecessary and irrelevant.

Yet polygamy continues to be banned even though it preserves the honor and chastity of women. In Western societies men prefer to keep polygamy illegal because it absolves them of responsibility. Legalized polygamy would require them to spend for the maintenance of their additional wives and offspring while the status quo allows them to enjoy extra-marital affairs without economic consequence.

Granted, there is the problem of natural jealousy among wives.[67] However, they are encouraged to overcome it to the best of their ability on the principle of liking for others what one would like for oneself. If the first wife should find such a situation unbearable she has the option of requesting divorce. And an unmarried woman is not under obligation to accept the proposal of a man already married; she is free to decide for herself. In some societies, a wife will seek a second wife for her husband to be a companion for herself and share in some of her responsibilities.

Islam takes the society as a whole into consideration, seeking to maximize benefit and reduce harm. As long as there are certain individual and social problems whose solution lies in the taking of an additional wife, it cannot be prohibited. Yet, in spite of its legality most in Muslim countries, it is a small minority of Muslims that actually enter into a second marriage as most men cannot afford the expense of maintaining more than one family.

44. Why does Islam prohibit a woman from having more than one husband?

Some people question the logic of allowing Muslim men to have more than one spouse while denying the same 'right' to women. While almost every society has supported the concept of a man having more than one woman, seldom has any social order ever supported the concept of a woman being married to two or more men at the same time.

---

[67] Yet no one has cited jealousy among siblings as a reason not to have another child.

The foundation of an Islamic society is justice and equity. God created men and women equal as human beings but not identical in nature. They have innate differences physiologically and psychologically, and have different capabilities. Hence, their roles and responsibilities may differ, but they serve to complement one another.

Feminists might object to the male's right to more than one wife by insisting that women should also be able to practice polyandry.[68] However, the following few points should be considered:

- As mentioned earlier, one of the benefits of polygamy is that it deals with the problem of women outnumbering men. Conversely, polyandry would only add to this problem if several men, who are already in shortage, were to marry one of the women, who are in abundance.

- In general, men are more polygamous by nature than women and have greater sexual needs.

- Islam assigns great importance to the recognition of both parents. When a man has more than one wife, the parents of children born in the marriage can easily be identified. But in the case of a woman marrying more than one husband, only the mother of the children would be known. How would a child of such a marriage know who his father was without resorting to laboratory tests? Would he accept his mother identifying the father by some chance method? Although recent advances in science have made it possible for both the mother and father to be identified through genetic testing, for a married woman to have to inquire who the father of her child is in order to register him in school or get medical care seems impractical, to say the least. In addition,

---

[68] i.e., marriage to more than one husband.

psychologists tell us that children who do not know their parents, the father in particular, undergo mental disturbances and trauma, and often have unhappy childhoods.

• Biologically, it is not difficult for a man to perform his duties as a husband despite having several wives. But a woman having several husbands would find it very difficult if not impossible to perform all her duties as a wife to each one of them. Complying when each husband desired intimacy with her at various times, keeping house for each one and looking after all of their children would undoubtedly be problematical.

These issues should be obvious to every intelligent person. Moreover, it has now been medically proven that one of the major causes of the serious diseases which have become so widespread is women having intercourse with more than one man and the mixing of seminal fluids in the womb. Hence, the Qur'an has prescribed a waiting period for the woman who has been divorced or widowed, so that enough time passes for her womb to be cleansed of any traces of the former husband before she marries again.

45. How can a Muslim be happy?

Happiness is a feeling that resides in the heart. It is characterized by peace of mind, tranquility, a sense of well-being and a relaxed disposition. From an Islamic perspective, it is of two levels: worldly pleasure and eternal happiness.

A believer's focus is usually more on eternal happiness, although it does not mean that Muslims forfeit the good things of the present life. Islam does not deny the importance of material causes for enjoyment, except that they are not an essential requirement for it; material things are merely among the means that might contribute to it. The Shari'ah lays down a number of directives and guidelines to secure man's happiness during his life on earth, and at the same time, Islam teaches that the benefits of this world may be used as a means to attain happiness in the eternal life of the Hereafter by sharing them with others and showing gratitude to God.

A Muslim finds his greatest happiness and contentment in his faith, and this certainly applies to the present life as well as the next. Someone who believes in God with a belief that is pure and free from any defects will enjoy a tranquil heart, a peaceful soul and will be pleased with whatever God has provided for him. Submission to the will of God (which is the meaning of "Islam") gives a believer the peace of mind needed in order to be industrious and persevering. Aware that his life has meaning and a definite purpose, he is motivated to expend effort in order to realize it. His enhanced perception of the moments, hours, and days of his life leaves no place for boredom or depression.

Faith also protects a Muslim against the causes of unhappiness. A believer is mentally prepared to accept patiently whatever God should decree for him. He knows that he will be tried and tested throughout his life, and additionally, that those trials are opportunities for him to put his faith into practice and earn rewards not proportionate to, but many times greater than his suffering. Such tests help him to develop inner strength through patience and determination, trusting in God, seeking His assistance, and fearing Him alone.

The life of this world fluctuates between periods of ease and difficulty, just as an individual does from health to illness or from wealth to need and vice versa. Additionally, man is a social being who needs to interact with others of his own kind. Because individuals differ in their physical and mental qualities it is unavoidable that there will be some displeasing occurrences among them causing sorrow and distress. If people cannot deal with problems in an evenhanded and principled manner their dealings with others can become a great source of misery. For this reason, Islam emphasizes the development of strong moral character and endeavors to develop in its followers a balanced and harmonious emotional makeup and eliminate such negative manners as anger, pride, conceit, stinginess, envy, and malice which lead to anxiety and emotional instability.

A person's satisfaction with another depends largely on the esteem he holds for him. God is the greatest source of peace for the heart, and remembering Him brings pleasure, comfort and joy to the soul of a believer. It connects the believer to his Creator, so that he sees beyond the world around him. Consequently, he does not overrate the importance of worldly occurrences so much that they disturb his spirit.

The believer constantly deals with the trials throughout his life by practicing patience, determination, courage, hard work, proper behavior and reliance upon God. He avoids that which causes spiritual malady and weakness: following vain desires, clinging to baseless beliefs, excessive devotion to pleasure, etc., because such things corrupt the heart and endanger the soul. Islam is also concerned with man's physical health and well-being; hence it forbids the consumption of anything that is hazardous to the body or can diminish or cause harm to the mind.

Because Muslims are serious about their religion, people sometimes ask if they are allowed to enjoy themselves. But who said there is no enjoyment in Islam? Muslims enjoy themselves within the framework of all that

God has permitted and feel no regret for missing the few things He prohibited, knowing that they must be harmful in some way. There is no true enjoyment in doing something God has prohibited either, because sin is always followed by a sense of discomfort. A Muslim is content with the countless blessings, apparent and unapparent, that his Creator has bestowed upon him and deeply appreciates that he has been guided to the best life in both worlds. This is the true happiness of which millions of people are deprived.

Anyone who would like to know more about happiness should read some accounts by people who have entered Islam, consider the great changes that occurred in their lives and the contentment they enjoy now. It is enjoyment that everyone should seek.

Warfare and Terrorism

46. Why are so many Muslims fundamentalists and extremists?

This question is often thrown at Muslims, directly or indirectly, during discussions on religion or world affairs due to the fact that false stereotypes and misinformation about Islam and Muslims are disseminated in the media.

"Islamic extremism" is being repeated incessantly by journalists, writers and politicians in an attempt to define things from their own particular perspective. The word "extremist" implies that someone stands far away from the accepted central norm, meaning that he is immoderate, a label that obviously gives expression to negative feelings.

Extremism is something blameworthy in Islam, as it means deviation from the moderation of Islamic teachings or from the correct method of applying them. Although the extremist might present his arguments from an Islamic point of view or be motivated by religious feelings, it remains an unacceptable position according to the Qur'an and guidance of Prophet Muhammad. Consequently, it has been condemned by all reliable Muslim scholars.

Extremism is bred by oppression. The most fertile environment for its proliferation is one where people are persecuted, repressed and denied their natural human rights, making them fearful, angry and emotionally unstable. In spite of this, Muslims are prohibited from allowing emotion to govern their behavior or acting on their own understanding of religious texts. Rather, they are under strict obligation to take their guidance from qualified scholars regarding the interpretation of those texts and their application to critical contemporary situations.

A great deal of attention has been given in Western media recently to the "threat of Islamic fundamentalism." The term "fundamentalist" reflects an intent to stigmatize those Muslims who adhere to the basic fundamental principles of Islam and pattern their lives accordingly. While a practicing Jew is called "orthodox" and a practicing Christian, Hindu or Buddhist "devout," a practicing Muslim is often referred to as a "fundamentalist."

So what, exactly, is a fundamentalist? It is someone who strictly adheres to the fundamental principles of his religion or his profession. For example, to be a good doctor one must know and practice the fundamentals of medicine. To be a good mathematician, one must know and practice the fundamentals of mathematics. Similarly, to be a good

Muslim one must know and practice the fundamentals of Islam.

The fundamentals of Islam include all noble qualities such as honesty, sincerity, chastity, generosity, and compassion. And they include the moderation which God has enjoined. A true Muslim is pleased to be a fundamentalist because he knows that the fundamentals of Islam are beneficial to the human race as a whole. If one analyzes the teachings of Islam with an open mind, he cannot escape the fact that they are full of benefits both for individuals and their societies.

47. Doesn't Islam promote terrorism, making it a threat to the world?

Terrorism is when innocent people are specifically targeted to instill fear in a population. It is categorically prohibited in Islam. The present era of our history has been blemished by indiscriminate violence in almost every society. The loss of innocent life has become extremely commonplace. Unfortunately, due to the actions of some ignorant Muslims as well as biased reporting in the media, the religion of Islam has come to be associated with terrorism. However, the appropriate question to be asked is: "Do Islamic teachings promote terrorism?"

As a matter of fact, Islam and terrorism are precise opposites; the very name, Islam, denotes peace and submission. The fundamentals of Islam direct its followers to maintain and promote peace throughout the world. Islam is a faith of moderation; thus a righteous and God-fearing Muslim can neither be a fanatic nor an extremist. There is no connection whatsoever between Islam and the violence practiced by terrorist groups in different parts of the world. In no way does it condone hijackings, hostage taking and the torture and killing of innocent people in order to achieve particular goals.

The Islamic basis for national and international relations is peace rather than war. Prominent Muslims, Islamic organizations and Islamic scholars have repeatedly denounced terrorist attacks and terrorism in general. Islam emphatically prohibits and disassociates itself from the violent acts that have been carried out by some of its members in the name of religion.

All religions and ideologies have some misguided followers, and it is surely unfair to judge any one of them by the behavior of such people. Accordingly, Islam should not be judged by the acts of misguided Muslims or even by the obvious corruption that permeates many Muslim countries. For in fact, what Islam teaches is one thing and what these so-called Muslims practice is something else. The only way to know the truth about Islam is to study its teachings, for they are the standard by which the actions of Muslims can be assessed as being right or wrong.

Islam emphasizes the sanctity of life in general, and particularly human life. And the Qur'an prohibits murder in clear terms:

"And do not kill the soul which Allah has forbidden [to be killed] except by [legal] right."[69]

"Whoever kills a soul unless for a soul[70] *or for corruption [done] in the land*[71] *– it is as if he had slain mankind entirely. And whoever saves one – it is as if he had saved mankind entirely."*[72]

---

[69] 5:32.
[70] i.e., in legal retribution for murder.
[71] i.e., that requiring the death penalty.
[72] 6:151.

Such is the value of a single human life, that God equates the unjust taking of one life with killing all of humanity. Only a proper and competent court can decide whether an individual has forfeited his right to life by commission of a major crime. Individual Muslims can never take decisions about who should be killed or punished. Conviction and punishment may not be implemented except by a qualified judge under lawful authority.

Terrorism involves the indiscriminate use of force to achieve certain objectives, and in reality it manifests itself in various forms. The head of state who orders the bombing of entire cities, the councils that kill millions of civilians by imposition of sanctions and the wealthy nations that would rather destroy their surplus food than make it available to those afflicted by famine are rarely punished for crimes against humanity.

Although it is recognized that Islamic history was not always filled with virtue, one should justly compare the number of civilians killed by Muslims to the number killed by communists and the western nations who ignited two world wars within half a century, deployed the atomic bomb against a civilian population, are currently supporting the brutal Israeli military occupation of Palestine against its civilians and have brought about the destruction of Iraq while thoroughly terrorizing its citizens.

While Islam seeks to promote peace it also directs its followers to oppose oppression. Both these objectives may on occasion require the use of force. It is precisely for this reason that police use force against criminals and anti-social elements to maintain law and order in society. So Islam does allow taking up arms under particular circumstances. Any civilization that did not could never survive. However, it prohibits the slightest injustice, even toward those who oppose the religion. The Qur'an orders:

> *"And do not let the hatred of a people prevent you from being just. Be just; that is nearer to righteousness."*[73]

Enmity toward any people or nation should not provoke Muslims to commit aggression against them or disregard their rights. As for the spread of Islam, this is supposed to take place peacefully by disseminating the message through the written and spoken word.

48. Wasn't Islam spread by the sword?

Some people claim that Islam would not have millions of adherents all over the world if it had not been spread by military force. Many school textbooks contain the picture of an Arab on horseback with the Qur'an in one hand and a sword in the other, symbolizing forcible conversion to the religion.

It has never been permitted to compel people to enter Islam by the use of weapons or any other means. If Islam was spread by the sword, then it was the sword of intellect and convincing arguments, the inherent force of truth, reason and logic – something which conquers the hearts and minds of people everywhere. Far from being spread by the sword, Islam has always accorded respect and freedom of choice to people of all faiths. The Qur'an instructs:

> *"There shall be no compulsion in [acceptance of] the religion. The right course has become clear from the wrong."*[74]

---

[73] 5:8.
[74] 2:256.

"Invite to the way of your Lord with wisdom and good instruction, and argue with them in a way that is best."[75]

The facts speak for themselves:

• Indonesia has the largest number of Muslims in the world, and the majority of people in Malaysia are Muslims. But no Muslim army ever went into Indonesia or Malaysia. Muslim traders and educators carried the message of God to those regions and impressed people as outstanding models of honesty and morality.

• Similarly, Islam spread rapidly on the East Coast of Africa although no Muslim army was ever dispatched to East Africa.

• Despite the disappearance of Islamic rule from many regions of Asia and Africa, their people have remained Muslims. This shows that the effect of Islam is one of approval and moral conviction, quite in contrast to that of western colonial occupation which left its formerly subjugated peoples with painful memories of exploitation, affliction and oppression.

• Muslims ruled Spain for over 800 years. It is a documented historical fact that during this period Christians and Jews enjoyed freedom to practice their respective religions. But thereafter, under Christian Spain, Muslims and Jews were subjected to tribunals of inquisition and torture.

• There was no "sword of Islam" held over non-Muslim minorities in Muslim countries. Until fairly recently Christian and Jewish minorities have lived peacefully with

---

[75] 16:125.

their Muslim neighbors in the Middle East.[76] If Muslims had made use of the sword there would no longer be Arabs of other religions.

• Because Islamic law protects the status of minorities, places of worship belonging to other faiths are found throughout the Muslim world. Islamic law also allows non-Muslim minorities to set up their own courts to implement family laws drawn up by the minorities themselves. The lives and properties of all citizens, whatever their religion, must be safeguarded by an Islamic government.

• Muslims ruled India for 800 years, during which they possessed enough power and authority to force all the people to convert to Islam. But they did not do so, and thus, more than 80% of the population remains non-Muslim.

• Worldwide statistics for the period from 1934 to 1984 show that adherents to Islam had increased by 235%, while adherents to Christianity had increased by 47%. There was obviously no Islamic conquest during that fifty-year period.

• The fastest growing religion in America and Europe today is Islam in spite of the fact that Muslims in these lands are still small minorities. The only sword they have in their possession is the sword of truth. It is this sword which is converting people to Islam.

49. Isn't Islam a militant religion?

Among the biggest misconceptions about Islam is that it is a militant religion. A few verses from the Qur'an are often quoted out of context by its opponents or by those who know little about it in order to perpetuate the myth that Islam

---

[76] The sectarian animosity of recent times has been stirred up largely by political injustices rather than matters of religion.

promotes violence, bloodshed and brutality and exhorts Muslims to kill non-believers.

To cite one example, would-be detractors usually quote from the Qur'an: ***"Then kill the polytheists wherever you find them."*** But in order to understand these words it is necessary to put them back into their proper context. After several military campaigns in which the pagans of Makkah attempted to annihilate the Muslims, a peace agreement was drawn up between the two sides. The pagans soon violated this treaty, so the Muslim army was instructed to resume combat against those who were fighting them. In light of the historical context of these words, an unbiased person would certainly agree that they cannot be used as proof that Islam promotes violence or orders the killing of anyone outside its fold.

The people being referred to in this verse are the pagan Arabs who had been waging war against the Prophet and who had broken their covenant and treaties with him. The verse is not speaking about other pagan Arabs who did not break their treaties and take up arms against Muslims. And most definitely it is not speaking about the Jews, Christians or the pagans outside of Arabia.

The verse that follows, which is conveniently ignored by the adversaries, completes the picture:

"If any one of the polytheists asks you for asylum, then grant him asylum so that he may hear the words of Allah [i.e., the Qur'an]. Then deliver him to his place of safety. That is because they are a people who do not know."[77]

What army general today would direct his soldiers to spare an enemy during a battle and then escort him to a place of

---

[77] 9:6.

safety? But this is what God has instructed in the Qur'an. Islam keeps warfare at a level of mercy and respect for the enemy unlike that of any other system. It orders that armies deal with the enemy justly even on the battlefield, and has drawn a clear line of distinction between combatants and non-combatants in enemy territory. Prophet Muhammad instructed his armies, "Do not kill any old person, child or woman"[78] and do not kill monks in monasteries."[79] For those enemies active in combat and those taken as prisoners of war, the list of rights is lengthy. There should be no torture, no killing of the wounded and defenseless and no mutilation of enemy corpses. Had the purpose of battle been to force unbelievers to accept Islam, the Prophet would never have commanded the Muslims to refrain from hostilities once the enemy had relented and would not have prohibited the killing of priests and monks.

Moreover, Islam permits war only in specific and critical circumstances as a last resort when all other attempts at obtaining peace and justice have failed. This is indeed the logical option for any nation. Western countries themselves defend the necessity of war to implement or maintain peace and do not regard it as a dangerous evil.

Muhammad was a prophet of mercy, but he was compelled to turn to battle when certain powers refused mercy and morality and sought to deprive others of them. Sometimes he had to fight for the mere survival of his mission. But the total number of days the Prophet was required to spend in defensive warfare comes to less than a year and his most famous battles did not last for more than one day. Once security was ensured, he immediately reverted to peace and diplomacy.

---

[78] Narrated by Abu Dawud.
[79] Narrated by Ahmad.

The Qur'an clearly says:

> *"Fight in the cause of Allah those who fight you, but do not commit aggression. Indeed, Allah does not like aggressors."*[80]
>
> *"And if they incline to peace, then incline to it [also] and rely upon Allah. Indeed, He is the Hearing, the Knowing."*[81]

Weapons can only be drawn against those who continue to persecute and oppress others and prevent them from following their own consciences in matters of belief. Even when they are compelled to fight and consequently conquer the land, their duty thereafter is to establish God's law and uphold justice for all people, Muslim and non-Muslim. It is not their right to coerce their subjects into accepting Islam. Non-Muslims are allowed to remain on their own faith and to practice it, although they are also expected to respect Islamic laws and not provoke unrest and disorder.

50. Then, what is the meaning of jihad?

"Jihad" is a term often misunderstood and associated with violent radical militants. This Arabic word is frequently mistranslated as "holy war," although there is no such thing in Islam. Holy war is something undertaken to forcibly subject others to certain religious doctrines. As we have seen, this is expressly forbidden in Islam.

The Arabic word "jihad" actually means a struggle or striving, and applies to any great effort on the personal as well as the social level. It is striving to do good and remove injustice and evil from oneself and from society. This exertion of effort can be spiritual, social, economic or

---

[80] 2:190.
[81] 8:61.

political. For example, one of the highest levels of jihad is to stand before a tyrant and speak a word of truth. Restraining the self from wrongdoing is also a form of jihad. It is a broad Islamic concept that includes opposing evil inclinations within the self, opposing injustice by peaceful means, the exertion of effort to improve the quality of life in society as well as the striving by military forces on a battlefield in defense of the community or of peoples oppressed. Jihad is not synonymous with war, as that is only one possible aspect of the term, and it certainly does not include terrorism.

Indeed, the concept of jihad is one of life, and it is vast, not limited only to armed conflict. One finds in the Qur'an mention of "jihad by means of the Qur'an,"[82] meaning invitation to truth using the best arguments, presentation of evidence and clarification. And there is jihad of the soul, which means striving to purify the soul, to increase its faith, incline it toward good and keep it away from evil. Then there is jihad through wealth, which means spending it in various beneficial ways, including charities and welfare projects. And there is jihad through the self, which comprises all good works done by a believer.

It includes the protection of societies from oppression, foreign domination and dictatorships that usurp rights and freedom, that abolish just and moral rule, that prevent people from hearing the truth or following it, and that practice religious persecution. Jihad endeavors to teach belief in the one supreme God and worship of Him, to spread good values, virtue and morality through wise and proper methods. Jihad means striving for social reform and the elimination of ignorance, superstition, poverty, disease and racial discrimination. Among its main objectives is securing

---

[82] Refer to 25:52

rights for weaker members of society against the impositions of the powerful and influential.

Armed jihad is not an option for Muslim individuals or groups. It can only be declared by the Muslim head of state and religious leadership. Moreover, it must never be fought for worldly gain, conquest or revenge. Muslims may only engage in battle to protect peoples' lives, properties and freedom.

Islam and War

Although jihad is a wider concept than war, it is also clear that Islam acknowledges armed struggle when there is no other option for the treatment of such problems as oppression and aggression and the defense of legitimate freedoms and rights. Its purpose is not to convert people to the religion, nor is it to colonize or acquire land and wealth. When Islam permits military engagement it is as an integral part of a complete system of values inherent in the religion, behind which any equitable person can perceive reason and logic.

War becomes jihad only when it is waged for the acceptance of God and according to the laws of God. Even self defense will not be considered jihad if Muslims are striking back in revenge. While Islam encourages oppressed people to strive for liberation and orders Muslims to help those who are oppressed, under no circumstance does it allow indiscriminate killing and terrorizing, destruction of homes, animals and crops or the torture of prisoners.

Jihad has conditions of restraint that distinguish it from any other kind of warfare. They can be summarized as follows:

- Muslims may not begin hostilities. They must strive for peace as much as possible.

- All treaties and agreements must be observed as long as the enemy continues to observe them.
- Muslims must fight only those who fight against them; non-combatants are not to be harmed.
- Weapons of mass destruction must never be used and collective punishment is strictly prohibited.
- Hostilities should be ended as soon as the other party is inclined to peace.

Throughout their history Muslims have entered battles and armed conflicts under these terms. If the situation is different today, it is only because these Islamic principles are not being observed.

When all peaceful means such as dialogue, negotiations and agreements have failed and an Islamic government chooses the option of war, it must be confined to the divinely ordained system that is precise, just, teaches proper ethics in the situation of war and provides opportunity for peace. The conditions that indicate the kind of warfare lawful to Muslims as a form of jihad show clearly that Islam does not condone aggression against anyone.

Finally .....

Dear reader, we now have a few simple questions to ask you. Did you ever wonder ....

- Why is a Jew practicing his religion called orthodox, a Christian practicing his called devout, but when a Muslim practices his religion he is labeled a fundamentalist?

- Why can a nun be covered from head to toe and be respected for devoting herself to God, but when a Muslim woman does that, she's considered fanatic or oppressed?
- Why, when a non-Muslim steals, rapes or murders, his religion is irrelevant, but when a Muslim is charged with a crime, it is Islam that goes on trial?
- Why has Prophet Muhammad been singled out in Western media for abuse and criticism?

But then again, why, in spite of so many negative portrayals, is Islam the fastest growing religion in the world?

We would now like our readers to ask themselves what they think are the reasons for all the propaganda and misinformation being spread around. If Islam was just another false religion that made no sense would so many people need to invent so many falsehoods about it?

Our answer is merely that the ultimate truth of Islam stands on unshakeable ground and that its basic fundamental belief in one supreme God is above reproach. Hence, because no one can criticize its doctrines directly, opponents can only resort to spreading misinformation about Islam so that people will be deterred from it and lose the desire to find out more.

This religion comes from God and it is protected by Him. If any other religion had been exposed to the wars, conspiracies and plots that Islam has been exposed to, it would have been dispensed with long ago or essentially altered as other religions have been. This faith, however, has remained unchanged for over 1400 years, while love of it constantly renews itself in the hearts of its followers and adherence to it increases with their increase in education and knowledge – further evidence that it is truly God's religion.

Islam provides mankind with a reason to live and with an ethical code by which to live. It outlines the dimensions of universal relationships – with individuals, societies and all of creation. It protects the institution of the family, upholds principles of justice, self-sufficiency, personal and collective responsibility, freedom of thought. Islam provides the foundations for a stable society, progress, security and world peace.

If more Muslims were to present Islam correctly and clearly it would surely make many people reconsider and re-evaluate their own beliefs. It is quite likely that both scholars and lay people, upon finding a universal religion that teaches people to worship God and respect His prophets within a framework of pure monotheism, would at least feel the need to reassess the basis for their own beliefs and doctrines. And it is that to which all people are invited by the Qur'an.

Yes, Islam is the fastest growing religion in the world today, and it has the answer to problems facing the modern world. Do not judge the religion by what you see on television or by what some Muslims or so-called Muslim leaders are doing. Study it from its authentic sources and speak to sincere practicing Muslims. You will surely find a different picture than that projected by the media. You may even find that Islam is what you have been looking for all your life.

May God guide you to the truth.

References

Abd-Allah, A., *The Qur'an, Knowledge and Science*, USC-MSA Compendium of Muslim Texts Website, www.usc.edu/dept/MSA

Abul-Fadl, Mona, *Introducing Islam from Within*, Leicester, UK, The Islamic Foundation, 1991.

AbuSulayman, Abdul-Hamid A., *Crisis in the Muslim Mind*, Herndon, USA, The International Institute of Islamic Thought, 1993.

Ali, Mary C., *The Question of Hijab: Suppression or Liberation?*, The Institute of Islamic Information and Education, Chicago, USA.

Estes, Yusuf, *Islam Tomorrow Website*, www.islamtomorrow.com

Maududi, S. Abul-A'la, *The Meaning of the Qur'an*, Lahore, Islamic Publications Ltd, 1979.

al-Munajjid, Muhammad Salih, *Islam QA Website*, www.islam-qa.com

Naik, Dr. Zakir Abdul Karim, *Islamic Research Foundation Website*, ww.irf.net

al-Oadah, Dr. Salman bin Fahd, *Islam Today Website*, www.islamtoday.com

al-Qaradawi, Yusuf, *Islamic Awakening Between Rejection and Extremism*, Herndon, USA, International Institute of Islamic Thought, 1995.

Qutb, Muhammad, *Islam the Misunderstood Religion*, Kuwait, International Islamic Federation of Student Organizations, 1977.

Qutb, Sayyid, *The Islamic Concept and Its Characteristics*, www.islambasics.com

Ṣaḥeeḥ International, *Introducing Islam*, Jeddah, Abul-Qasim Publishing House, 1995.

Ṣaḥeeḥ International, *The Qur'an – Arabic Text with Corresponding English Meanings*, Jeddah, Abul-Qasim Publishing House, 1997.

al-Sheha, Abdul-Rahman, *Human Rights in Islam and Common Misconceptions* Riyadh, www.islamland.org

Umm Muhammad, *In the Light of Surah an-Nur,* Jeddah, Abul-Qasim Publishing House, 2005.

Umm Muhammad, *The Global Messenger*, Riyadh, The International Program for Introducing the Prophet of Mercy, 2006.

www.ingramcontent.com/pod-product-compliance
Lightning Source LLC
LaVergne TN
LVHW012000070526
838202LV00054B/4989